The Beekeeping Bible

The Comprehensive Guide for Beginner Beekeepers - Building Your Hive, Caring for Bees, Harvesting Honey, and Exploring Profitable Opportunities

Roberta Bird

The Beekeeping Bible
© Copyright 2023 by Roberta Bird
All rights reserved

This document is geared towards providing exact and reliable information with regards to the topic and issue covered. The publication is sold with the idea that the publisher is not required to render accounting, officially permitted, or otherwise, qualified services. If advice is necessary, legal or professional, a practiced individual in the profession should be ordered. From a Declaration of Principles which was accepted and approved equally by a Committee of the American Bar Association and a Committee of Publishers and Associations. In no way is it legal to reproduce, duplicate, or transmit any part of this document in either electronic means or in printed format. Recording of this publication is strictly prohibited and any storage of this document is not allowed unless with written permission from the publisher.

All rights reserved.

The information provided herein is stated to be truthful and consistent, in that any liability, in terms of inattention or otherwise, by any usage or abuse of any policies, processes, or directions contained within is the solitary and utter responsibility of the recipient reader. Under no circumstances will any legal responsibility or blame be held against the publisher for any reparation, damages, or monetary loss due to the information herein, either directly or indirectly. Respective authors own all copyrights not held by the publisher. The information herein is offered for informational purposes solely, and is universal as so. The presentation of the information is without contract or any type of guarantee assurance. The trademarks that are used are without any consent, and the publication of the trademark is without permission or backing by the trademark owner. All trademarks and brands within this book are for clarifying purposes only and are the owned by the owners themselves, not affiliated with this document.

TABLE OF CONTENTS

CHAPTER 1: INTRODUCTION TO BEEKEEPING 1

The Importance of Beekeeping 1

Understanding Bee Behavior 4

Benefits of Beekeeping 7

Challenges in Beekeeping 9

Beekeeping and the Environment 13

CHAPTER 2: THE ESSENTIALS OF BEEKEEPING 17

Types of Bees 17

Beekeeping Equipment 19

Choosing Your Bee Breed 22

Suiting Up for Safety 25

Understanding Beekeeping Laws and Regulations 27

CHAPTER 3: BUILDING YOUR FIRST HIVE 31

Choosing the Right Location 31

Types of Beehives 33

Constructing Your Hive 36

Preparing Your Hive for Bees 38

Introducing Bees to Your Hive 41

CHAPTER 4: CARING FOR YOUR BEES 45

Monitoring Your Hive 45

Feeding Your Bees 47

Managing Pests and Diseases 49

Bee Health and Colony Collapse Disorder 52

Winterizing Your Hive 54

CHAPTER 5: THE LIFE CYCLE OF BEES 59

The Role of the Queen Bee 59

The Role of Worker Bees 61

The Role of Drones 64

Understanding Swarming 66

The Importance of Pollination 69

CHAPTER 6: THE ART OF BEEKEEPING 73

Beekeeping Seasons 73

Managing Multiple Hives 75

Splitting and Transferring Hives 77

Attracting Bees to Your Garden 80

Bee-Friendly Plants 82

BONUS 1: AUDIOBOOK 85

BONUS 2: VIDEO 87

EXCLUSIVE BONUS: 3 EBOOK 89

AUTHOR BIO: ROBERTA BIRD 91

CHAPTER 1

INTRODUCTION TO BEEKEEPING

The Importance of Beekeeping

Keeping bees, or apiculture, may seem like a hobby for only the most dedicated enthusiasts. But the practice of beekeeping offers benefits far beyond just harvesting honey. Honey bees play an integral role in plant pollination, enabling fruit and vegetable crops to thrive. By cultivating local honey bee colonies, beekeepers directly support critical pollinator populations that contribute to our food systems and biodiversity.

Honey bees are the most economically valuable pollinators we have. As generalized pollinators, honey bees visit a diverse range of flowering plants. In doing so, they transfer pollen between flowers to enable fertilization and the production of fruits, vegetables, nuts, and seeds. It is estimated that one third of the food we eat relies on insect pollination, with bees pollinating over 90 different crops. The bountiful yields provided by bee pollination are valued at over $15 billion per year in the United States alone. Crops such as apples, almonds, blueberries, cherries, avocados, onions, broccoli, and alfalfa either fully depend on or produce significantly higher yields with honey bee pollination. By supporting these essential agricultural pollinators, beekeepers indirectly contribute to food security.

Beyond agriculture, honey bees also pollinate wild flowering plants. This facilitates ecosystem biodiversity, as diverse plant communities form the foundation of thriving habitats for other wildlife species. From deserts to forests to backyard gardens, honey bees help enable ecological richness wherever they fly. Protecting honey bee populations is therefore important not just for agriculture but for conservation efforts.

In recent years, beekeepers have observed alarming rates of honey bee colony losses. This decline threatens the pollination services bees provide. Colony collapse disorder and other rising threats like Varroa mites, diseases, pesticides, and climate change have been linked to widespread overwintering colony losses. Urban development also reduces available nesting habitats for bees. Given these mounting stressors on honey bee health, intentional beekeeping has become crucial to sustaining bee populations locally.

Backyard beekeepers provide managed colonies with ideal hive conditions, supplemental feeding, and active disease management. This supports honey bee survival and propagation. Having local hives ensures a stable presence of pollinators, even in areas with few wild bee habitats. Well-managed urban and suburban colonies can produce surplus honey while still meeting the colony's nutritional needs. Harvesting this excess honey gives the beekeeper a sweet reward. When done sustainably, extracting honey also prevents the hive from becoming honey bound. This occurs when bees fill comb cells completely with honey, leaving little room for brood rearing.

For the amateur beekeeper, a thriving hive becomes an enriching hands-on education into entomology. Opening up the hive offers an inside look under the veil into the fascinating social world of bees. Beekeepers get to observe the queen bee, workers, brood, honey stores and the comb up close. Seeing the intricate wax comb take shape and fill with honey is an intriguing privilege. Diagnosing and addressing any issues within the colony provides insight into how the superorganism functions. Troubleshooting problems together with the bees can create a sense of kinship through this collaboration. The more beekeepers learn, the better advocates they become for protecting bees holistically.

Of course, cultivating a new colony from scratch requires an investment of time, effort and adequate training. Novices should connect with local beekeeping groups to find a mentor. Reading books and taking a beekeeping course will lay the educational groundwork. Budgeting approximately $1,000 or more upfront will allow purchase of the woodware, protective gear, tools and bees necessary. Finding a suitable hive location partly in sun with suitable year-round forage within a few miles is also key. While challenging at times, keeping bees teaches principles of animal husbandry, agriculture and ecology through firsthand experience.

The natural seasonal cycle of the hive dictates much of the beekeeper's work. Building up the colony in spring, preventing swarming in summer, and overwintering bees in fall require different management tactics. Spring is focused on stimulating brood rearing as the colony rapidly expands. Adding extra boxes, or supers, to contain the honey stores gives bees adequate room. Monitoring for disease and queen issues is also important in spring. During the active summer months, strategies to prevent overcrowding and swarming are needed. Careful inspections help determine ideal timing to harvest surplus honey frames. Leaving sufficient honey stores for the colony's winter nutrition is essential. Come late fall, reducing hive entrances and wrapping hives helps conserve heat as the colony clusters for warmth. Feeding protein and carbohydrates can support winter health. Ongoing parasite monitoring and mitigation is critical year-round. With proper seasonal care tailored to their needs, colonies can successfully survive cold winters.

In many ways, beekeeping requires beekeepers to act as collaborative caretakers. Bees do not passively reside in artificial hives, but rather actively make it their home. Adjusting to the bees' needs and rhythms allows them to thrive. Cultivating a hive is not about rigid control, but rather balancing intentional care with flexibility. For instance, bees often propolis small interior gaps within their hive that beekeepers want to keep open. Yet this resinous "bee glue" helps regulate humidity and air flow as the bees desire; accommodating some propolis preserves hive harmony. With attentiveness and adaptation, beekeepers and bees can develop a synergistic relationship.

Above all, beekeeping teaches profound lessons about interconnectivity. The health of bees, plants, ecosystems, and our food systems are all interdependent. Caring for a single hive impacts vegetation at both local and landscape scales. Keeping bees also connects us to nature's cycles, seasons, and the origins of our food. By better understanding honey bees, we gain awareness that in turn informs global environmental stewardship. Whether done for personal education or large-scale agriculture, beekeeping has far-reaching implications. Our actions as beekeepers ripple outward, contributing to a mosaic of efforts needed to sustain honey bees and preserve biodiversity.

In summary, beekeeping serves essential ecological functions that extend beyond the apiary. Honey bees rank among the most economically and ecologically valuable pollinators, enabling diverse ecosystems and bountiful crops. But due to accumulating stresses, intentional bee stewardship is needed to revitalize struggling bee populations. As individual beekeepers help honey bees thrive, they collectively support global biodiversity, food security, and sustainable agriculture. The wisdom gained from tending hives generates observant advocates for protecting bees and our interconnected world. Though demanding, the work of beekeepers ultimately advances profound causes.

Understanding Bee Behavior

Bees are social insects that live in colonies consisting of three types of bees - the queen, workers, and drones. To operate as a cohesive unit, honey bees rely on complex methods of communication and intricate social interactions. Gaining an in-depth understanding of honey bee behavior provides critical insight for beekeepers on colony management.

The roles and responsibilities of each type of bee dictate their behaviors. The queen bee is the only fertile female in the colony capable of laying eggs. Her sole purpose is to reproduce, laying up to 2,000 eggs per day to maintain and expand the colony. The queen communicates through pheromones to signal her presence and fertility status to the rest of the colony. Worker bees assume all non-reproductive tasks, including foraging for food, building honeycomb, caring for the young, defending the hive, and maintaining the hive temperature. Their roles vary as they age, from cell cleaners in their first few days to foragers in their last weeks of life. Forager bees exhibit the most extensive set of complex behaviors as they search for pollen and nectar. Scout bees go out in search of new food sources, returning to the hive to communicate locations through waggle dances. Foragers then follow this information to productive locations. Drones exist only to mate with a virgin queen from another hive. They do not gather food, produce wax, or care for offspring.

Understanding how honey bees communicate enables beekeepers to recognize signs of colony health and issues. Honey bees primarily communicate through pheromones, body movements, and activities within the hive. The queen produces a pheromone that suppresses queen rearing and identifies her presence. A decline in this "queen substance" due to aging or death triggers emergency queen cells to be built. Forager bees communicate foraging locations to other workers through unique body movements called "dances." The waggle dance indicates direction and distance, while the round dance shows a food source is nearby. Bees also communicate through touch, odor, and food exchange. Understanding their communication methods allows beekeepers to detect things like preparation to swarm or notes of alarm through heightened activity levels.

Honey bee defense mechanisms also stem from inherent behaviors. Guard bees protect the hive entrance, assessing intruders through smell. Defending the colony is essential for survival. Bees respond to perceived threats by stinging, releasing pheromones that signal an attack, and swarming on the intruder. Africanized "killer" bees exhibit more intense defensive behaviors due to genetic traits that make them more aggressive. Knowledge of defensive responses enables beekeepers to use protective equipment and gentle handling techniques to avoid eliciting aggression.

The migratory nature of honey bees underpins key behaviors like swarming. In late spring, as the hive population grows, scouting bees search for new nesting sites. Swarming is the process where the old queen departs with a portion of worker bees to establish a new colony. Several virgin queens remain in the original hive to compete for dominance. A successful virgin will then embark on mating flights to collect enough sperm to fertilize eggs for years. Understanding swarming instincts enables prevention techniques like splitting strong hives before swarming starts.

Honey bees also exhibit complex social behaviors and communication methods. Young worker bees perform brood care, feeding larvae and cleaning cells. Older workers take on roles that support colony functioning like comb building, guarding, and foraging. House bees distribute food, remove dead bees, and regulate climate within the hive. This age-based division of labor is structured to meet the colony's needs. Bees also use trophallaxis to exchange food, communicating its nature, location, availability and urgency. The passing of nectar from foragers to house bees, then between house bees, enables efficient food dispersal.

There are a wide variety of factors that can influence honey bee behavior. Weather is one element - bees are less active on cloudy, windy, or cool days. The availability of flowers affects foraging behaviors. Times of scarcity lead to greater food sharing within the hive. A beekeeper's management techniques also impact activities like swarming and defensive responses. Understanding bee biology and typical behavioral patterns enables one to recognize anomalous behaviors that may signify issues. Sudden lethargy could indicate pesticide exposure or disease. Excessive defensive reactions can denote harassment or a lack of disease hygiene. Close observation is key to detecting abnormal behaviors requiring intervention.

In summary, honey bees display a range of behaviors intrinsic to their biological drives and roles within the colony. Their behaviors facilitate complex social interactions and efficient colony functioning. For beekeepers, making the effort to understand typical behavioral patterns better equips one to interpret the overall health and activities of the hive. Careful observation of in-hive activities, foraging behaviors, and bee-to-bee interactions provides insight on reproduction, food availability, disease prevalence and much more. A strong working knowledge of bee behavior allows for colonies to be managed in ways that support the fundamental needs of the hive.

Benefits of Beekeeping

Beekeeping provides numerous rewards for both the hobbyist and the environment. By learning the craft of apiculture, you can reap tangible benefits like honey production and pollination services while also finding personal fulfillment.

To start, tending to honey bees allows you to harvest fresh, natural honey for your own use. Once your colony is established, the excess honey can be extracted from frames and jars several times per year. This sweet treat has unmatched flavor and nutritional value straight from the hive. You'll come to appreciate the subtle tastes that vary by season, flower source, and regional climate. Sharing your honey with friends and family or even selling it can be immensely gratifying. Beyond eating it, you'll find versatile uses for beeswax like candles, cosmetics, wood treatments, artisan goods, and more. With some colonies producing over 60 pounds of surplus honey annually, you'll have plenty to enjoy.

You can also benefit from increased pollination in your garden and surrounding landscape when you keep bees. Bees play a vital role in pollinating over two-thirds of leading food crops. By situating hives nearby, your flowers, fruits, vegetables, and herbs will thrive thanks to greater pollen transfer. Your bee colonies essentially provide free pollination services that translate to higher agricultural yields. This makes beekeeping valuable for home gardeners and farmers alike. Whether you're cultivating a small urban plot or acres of rural farmland, your bees will enhance pollination and productivity.

Additionally, studying honey bee biology and behavior through beekeeping can be intellectually stimulating. You'll gain insight into one of nature's most complex and sophisticated social structures. Observing the hive's activity and division of labor can pique your curiosity. As you become attuned to external factors affecting your colony like weather, forage, and seasonal changes, you'll develop a deeper connection to the broader ecosystem. This hands-on experience fosters a greater appreciation for entomology, agriculture, and sustainability.

Beekeeping also encourages patience, care, and responsibility. Tending colonies requires diligence, yet rewards those willing to nurture their hives with tender loving care. You'll learn the art of beekeeping management, from regular inspections to disease prevention measures. With time, your colonies will even develop unique personalities. The bonds you form can bring profound personal fulfillment. There's deep satisfaction in guiding your hive successfully through each season and year.

This hobby can also benefit your local community, both environmentally and economically. Healthy honey bee populations are essential for wild plant conservation, home garden success, and sustainable agriculture. By actively managing bee colonies, you directly contribute to bolstering local pollinator numbers. That in turn helps fertilize native vegetation, provide food for wildlife, and pollinate neighbors' crops. Your surplus honey and hive products can even be sold at farmers markets or to restaurants, generating supplemental income while supplying your community with an artisanal local product.

For many beekeepers, this practice becomes a beloved, rewarding lifelong passion. Working with bees encourages ecological awareness and forges a special connection with nature. You'll gain practical skills and a sense of purpose tending to your colonies. The intellectual engagement and emotional bonds make beekeeping deeply meaningful on a personal level. Involvement with a local beekeeping association lets you network with and learn from experienced mentors too. You'll discover an inspiring community unified by knowledge, creativity, and appreciation for the natural world.

To summarize, beekeeping offers multifaceted benefits:

- Harvesting honey, beeswax, propolis, and other hive products
- Boosting crop yields through increased pollination
- Developing a scientific understanding of apiology and ecology
- Fostering patience, responsibility, and caregiving skills
- Promoting local biodiversity and environmental health
- Producing natural products to benefit family, friends, or income
- Finding personal fulfillment through connection with nature
- Building relationships and knowledge by engaging with a community of beekeepers

With proper guidance and attentive care, a single hive can provide you with these valuable rewards for many seasons. Though beekeeping entails dedication and effort, the benefits far outweigh the required work. The learning process is educational and often becomes a treasured hobby. The tangible products and services also make maintaining honey bees a worthwhile investment. By reaping these diverse benefits, you'll grow as a beekeeper, gardener, environmentalist, and individual.

Challenges in Beekeeping

Beekeeping comes with its fair share of challenges. Though keeping bees can be hugely rewarding, there are various difficulties and pitfalls to manage. Being aware of common issues ahead of time helps beekeepers prepare properly and prevent setbacks.

One of the biggest challenges in beekeeping is coping with colony health issues. Bees face numerous diseases and parasites, with viral infections, fungal infections, and Varroa mites being among the most common. These afflictions weaken and kill off bees, negatively impacting the hive. Identifying and treating such conditions early is crucial but difficult for beginners. Recognizing subtle disease symptoms takes attentive inspection and familiarity with bee biology. Applying proper integrative pest management practices also involves a learning curve. Mitigating diseases requires vigilance in monitoring colony health, investing in quality disease-resistant bee stock, and using selective treatments as needed rather than a blanket approach.

Another major challenge is maintaining queen health and brood production. The queen bee is the center of the colony, responsible for laying fertilized eggs to propagate the hive. Issues like queenlessness or infertility can quickly destabilize a colony. Spotting when the queen is compromised or failing requires close observation during hive checks. Replacing the queen by introducing a new mated queen can resolve such issues. But doing so at the right time and ensuring acceptance by the hive is an acquired skill. Protecting the queen during manipulations is also key to avoid accidental injury. Providing supplemental feeding when resources are scarce helps ensure consistent brood rearing as well. Mastering queen issues and brood production dynamics takes continual learning and experience.

Managing feeding and nutrition is itself an area of difficulty. Bees need a constant supply of pollen and nectar. When floral resources are scarce, colonies can starve without adequate food stores or supplemental feeding. Strategic feeding prevents malnutrition and promote colony growth. Yet determining the proper feed recipe, timing, method, and amount takes practice. Under- or over-feeding can have negative consequences. Feeding too late risks colonies starving mid-winter. Learning to read the status of food stores and respond accordingly enables keepers to effectively supplement when needed.

Dealing with swarming instincts also poses a serious challenge. Swarming is the natural means of propagation for honey bee colonies. When conditions are optimal, the old queen leaves with a large portion of worker bees to establish a new nest elsewhere. However, this leads to a substantial loss of resources and population for the beekeeper. There are methods to deter or prevent swarming, but these require meticulous timing and intervention. Splitting robust colonies preemptively, ensuring adequate space as the hive expands, and replacing old queens are some approaches to maintaining stability. Even with preventative steps, swarms can still occur unexpectedly.

Harvesting honey and other hive products is also trickier than expected. Honey cannot be collected until frames are completely capped and cured. Identifying the optimal time to harvest takes keen observation. Using proper equipment and techniques is necessary as well to avoid damaging the comb and spilling honey. Extracting honey while ensuring sufficient colony stores requires precise coordination. Learning signs of a nectar flow ending allows keepers to leave adequate honey reserves. Other hive products like beeswax, propolis and pollen also require specialized handling to harvest sustainably.

Year-round pests pose another threat to hive health. Besides mites, common nuisances include wax moth, small hive beetle and bears. Employing traps, hive modifications and deterrents helps protect against infestations. But perfect prevention is difficult, so early detection of any pests through inspections is critical. Quick action is needed to contain most pest issues before they escalate. However, some pests like bears require unique solutions tailored to each apiary site.

The stresses of winter also challenge beekeepers to help their colonies adapt. Preparing hives for colder months involves proper ventilation, insulation and moisture control. Monitoring food stores and supplemental feeding are vital going into winter. Strategically placing hives in sheltered locations or building windbreaks can help minimize temperature extremes. Yet even with the best preparations, extreme cold snaps or extended periods without cleansing flights can tax bees. Experienced beekeepers know to expect some overwintering losses.

Of course, beekeepers themselves also face risks working with stinging insects. Defensive maneuvers like stinging are common when hives are opened. Minor stings come with the territory. Yet caution is warranted, as some individuals can have severe allergic reactions to venom. Beekeepers must remain constantly vigilant when handling bees. Specialized suits and veils are a necessary precaution. Still, stings will inevitably occur occasionally. Managing these risks while performing hive manipulations presents an ongoing challenge.

As highlighted above, beekeepers take on a number of responsibilities to overcome obstacles and keep colonies healthy. Meeting these challenges demands patience, ingenuity and adaptability. Every region and beekeeper will face a unique set of specific hurdles to overcome. But with commitment to education, preparation and care, most common difficulties can be resolved before causing colony failure. The learning process itself brings valuable lessons that strengthen beekeeping practices over time. Through active problem solving guided by wisdom and resilience, challenges transform into opportunities for growth.

In summary, beekeeping comes with expected difficulties, but the rewards make persevering through them worthwhile. Learning to identify issues early, respond promptly and adjust approaches prevents most problems from becoming insurmountable. Research, mentorship and hands-on experience equip beekeepers with the tools needed to prevail. Meeting the challenges of beekeeping is both realistic and manageable with dedication to best practices. The satisfaction of tending to thriving hives despite the obstacles faced makes success all the sweeter. Savvy beekeepers come to appreciate that challenges present chances to expand their skills and deepen the connections shared with their colonies.

Beekeeping and the Environment

Beekeeping and bees themselves have an intricate and vital relationship with the surrounding environment. Bees play an essential role in plant pollination and in turn, a healthy ecosystem supports thriving bee populations. For managed colonies, beekeepers must consider environmental factors to ensure productive hives. Understanding the interconnected nature of bees and their habitat enables beekeepers to make decisions that mutually benefit bees, native ecosystems, and agricultural yields.

As pollinators, bees sustain biodiversity in natural ecosystems. Bees fertilize flowers to produce seeds and fruits that sustain wildlife. Their pollination facilitates plant growth that stabilizes soil and prevents erosion. Bees pollinate around 85% of flowering plant species worldwide. The fruits, nuts, and seeds resulting from insect pollination make up over a third of global food production. Declining bee populations negatively impact ecosystems. With fewer bees, plant reproduction and diversity suffer. The loss of plant species and diminished vegetation disrupts entire food chains. Preserving bee populations is therefore critical for sustaining diverse and healthy ecosystems.

For managed hives, beekeepers must consider environment factors like weather, forage availability, agricultural chemicals, and more. Inclement weather can limit opportunities for cleansing flights and foraging. Extended periods of cold, heat, or heavy rain disrupt normal hive activity and growth. Lack of diverse and abundant floral sources also hinders colony development. Mono-crop agriculture has reduced the diversity of bees' natural diets. Urban development and habitat loss further restrict native foraging grounds. Beekeepers should locate hives near pesticide-free wildflower meadows, woodlands, orchards or other varied foraging sites. Avoiding agrichemical exposure boosts colony immunity and productivity.

Beekeepers can employ strategies to limit environmental stressors. Providing clean water sources supports temperature regulation in hot months. Creating sheltered hive locations shields bees from severe winds and rain. Strategic food supplementation augments nutritional shortfalls when forage is scarce. Best practice includes leaving ample honey stores for overwintering bees rather than maximizing honey harvesting. Fostering genetic diversity through requeening boosts colony resilience to novel diseases and toxins. Overall vigilance enables mitigation steps before environmental factors seriously threaten managed colonies.

In choosing hive locations, considerations should include sun exposure, wind patterns, soil type, water availability and forage access. Hives require full sun exposure, especially in the morning, to warm effectively. Avoid excess afternoon shade that inhibits ventilation. Face hives away from prevailing winds that could topple them over or chill bees. Well-draining soil prevents flooding, allows burial of disease pathogens and reduces moisture in the hive itself. A nearby clean water source supports cooling, diluting collected nectar and rearing brood. Ensure hives are within reach of abundant, diverse forage from spring to late fall. Position extra hives at varying sites to maximize natural foraging over wider terrain.

Beekeepers can also directly support the environment through sustainable practices. Using local bees adapted to native conditions improves survival. Providing undisturbed, natural habitat on property preserves native plants and wildlife. Organic management eliminates chemical contamination of bees, soil and waterways. Sustainable harvesting limits honey extraction to surplus stores, retaining enough food for colony health. Supporting ethical queen breeders preserves genetic stock. Practicing integrated pest management minimizes acaricide use that breeds resistant mites. Overall environmental stewardship should inform each beekeeping decision.

Contribution to agricultural yields is another environmental consideration. With pollination services, managed hives enable farmers to improve crop output for food production. Strategic hive placement adjacent to orchards, vegetable crops and other farms boosts pollination efficiency. Bringing hives to fields during peak bloom, known as migratory beekeeping, maximizes fruit and seed yield. The vital pollination service managed bees provide makes beekeeping an integral part of sustainable agriculture.

In turn, farmlands offer vital foraging resources to maintain strong colonies. Communication with farmers ensures hives are situated in pesticide-free zones. Early season orchard blooms provide an excellent protein source to rapidly expand colonies in spring. Summer vegetable and legume blossoms supply bees with diverse nutrition. For beekeepers not involved in commercial pollination contracts, coordinating with local farmers provides mutual benefit. The same holds true in residential areas – educating neighbors on hosting bee-friendly gardens brings thriving flowers close to home.

A colony's health directly reflects the quality of its environment. Contaminants, lack of forage and weather extremes all impose stress. Yet attentive beekeepers can take meaningful steps to counteract these issues. Providing clean water, strategic food supplementation, genetic diversity and integrated pest management enables resilience even in marginal environments. Education, habitat conservation and sustainable agriculture practices serve to facilitate optimal bee habitats. In return, productive pollinator populations support biodiverse ecosystems, bountiful farmlands and colony prosperity. The interdependent welfare of bees and their surroundings makes environmental protection intrinsic to beekeeping stewardship.

Roberta Bird

CHAPTER 2

THE ESSENTIALS OF BEEKEEPING

Types of Bees

When getting started in beekeeping, it's important to understand the different types of bees you'll encounter in your hives. While most novice beekeepers begin with the common honey bee, Apis mellifera, there are actually several bee species and even subspecies suited to apiculture.

The most widespread domesticated bee is the Western honey bee, Apis mellifera. This species encompasses many different geographic races or subspecies adapted to local environments, including Italian, Carniolan, Caucasian, and Russian honey bees. In North America, the Italian and Carniolan bees are most popular. The Italian honey bee is known for its light coloration and gentleness. It tends to build up colonies quickly in the spring and produces large honey yields. The Carniolan honey bee originated in cooler mountainous areas, giving it the benefits of overwintering well and requiring less food storage. But it builds up colonies more slowly.

Another species is the Eastern or Oriental honey bee, Apis cerana. This bee has several advantages in tropical climates, including resistance to some diseases and parasites that afflict A. mellifera. It is a major managed pollinator in parts of Asia. The Eastern honey bee produces less honey surplus than its Western counterpart, but may be favored for its resilience, low hive maintenance, and lack of swarming tendencies.

Within North America, there are also localized subspecies of the Western honey bee bred for specific traits. The Buckfast bee was developed in the early 1900s by crossing multiple European subspecies, seeking to combine desirable qualities like honey production, gentleness, disease resistance, and overwintering ability. The Russian honey bee is a hardy type first imported in the 1990s. It demonstrates increased disease resistance and the ability to thrive in cold climates.

Moving beyond honey bees, there are other bee species successfully managed for agricultural pollination, though they do not produce surplus honey. The blue orchard bee, Osmia lignaria, is an efficient pollinator of orchard crops like almonds, apples, and cherries. These gentle bees nest in small holes, making them easy to propagate simply by providing the proper habitat. Mason bees, genus Osmia, are also excellent orchard pollinators. Species like the hornfaced bee and leafcutter bee are likewise managed for their superior pollination abilities.

In addition to relying on bees specifically bred for apiculture, you may encounter native species around your hives. Bumblebees form small colonies, usually underground, and help pollinate crops and wildflowers. Sweat bees, plasterer bees, carpenter bees, digger bees, and many more all play ecological roles near your hive. Learning to identify common native bees will help you become a better steward by providing the habitats and forage they need. With awareness and protection, native pollinators can thrive alongside managed honey bees.

To summarize key points:

- The Western honey bee (Apis mellifera) is the most widespread domesticated bee, with many subspecies like Italian and Carniolan bees.

- The Eastern honey bee (Apis cerana) is a tropical species valued for traits like disease resistance.

- Selective breeding has produced locally-adapted subspecies such as the Russian and Buckfast honey bees.

- Orchard mason bees (Osmia spp.) are managed as specialist pollinators that do not make honey.

- Many native bee species contribute to crop and ecosystem pollination near hives.

- Choosing a suitable honey bee type involves considering climate, desired productivity, disease resistance, and other factors.

- Skillful beekeepers learn to work productively with multiple bee species for honey production and pollination.

Understanding the categories of bees you're likely to encounter will help you establish hives tailored to your environment. A diversity of bee types can coexist in relative harmony when each is provided with suitable forage and habitat. As you delve into beekeeping, be open minded about the many species that may aid your apiary goals. With experience, you'll become adept at working symbiotically with honey bees, native bees, and other important pollinators around your hives.

Beekeeping Equipment

Getting started in beekeeping requires obtaining some key pieces of equipment. The various components serve specific purposes to safely house and care for a colony of honey bees. While specialized hive tools and protective gear may seem unfamiliar at first, understanding the use of each item will ensure you have what's needed.

The most obvious requirement for any beekeeper is a protective bee suit or jacket. Bee suits are thickly woven to prevent stings through the fabric. They feature full body coverage, including long sleeves with elastic cuffs and a veiled hood. The mesh face veil provides crucial facial and neck protection while allowing visibility. Gloves are optional but recommended at least while you gain confidence handling bees. Leather gloves allow more dexterity when manipulating frames. With practice, some beekeepers opt to work gloveless for inspections, but always keep a pair handy. Complete protective coverage is vital when first starting out and anytime you'll be heavily disturbing the hive.

Moving underneath the veil, the actual structure housing the colony comes next. The full hive consists of stacked boxes, known as supers or hive bodies. Standard LANGSTROTH hives, named after their inventor, are the most common style. The bottom hive body contains the brood chamber where bees actively rear brood, store pollen, and cluster in winter. Honey supers are added above as the colony's population grows through summer. A telescoping outer lid and inner cover help regulate ventilation and moisture. 10 frame Langstroth boxes with pre-stamped wax foundations are well suited for beginners. You'll need one deep or two medium brood chambers, plus at least two honey supers, inner covers, and top covers to start off.

Inside the hive bodies, frames provide structural support for the bees to construct wax comb. Wooden frames hold removable foundations made of wax sheet or plastic. Bees draw out the comb, often guided by the foundation's cell pattern, to store honey and house brood. Langstroth hives use rectangular frames of specific dimensions to fit the boxes precisely. Frames facilitate easy, non-destructive inspections when manipulated properly. Having extra frames and foundations available as spares is recommended.

For safely accessing the interior of the hive, a smoker and hive tool will be essential components of your kit. The smoker disperses cool smoke over and around the bees to temporarily mask alarm pheromones. This divertive effect keeps bees calm and less prone to stinging while you briefly open the hive. Fueling a smoker with natural materials like burlap or pine needles allows gentle smoking. Light the smoker well in advance so it stays lit. The metal hive tool then aids opening the hive. The flat blade is used to loosen frames stuck down with propolis, the sticky resin bees use as glue. Inserting the hooked end helps gently pry frames for removal. With practice, smooth frame manipulation keeps disruptions brief.

Additional equipment will be useful for hive maintenance. A frame or jumbo grip makes lifting frames easier. Frame holders temporarily hold removed frames. Bee brushes gently nudge bees back where needed. Queen catchers allow isolating and moving the queen safely during inspections. Marking pens help track the queen's age by coloring her thorax. Entry reducers can shrink the hive entrance to defend against robbers. Screen bottom boards help monitor and manage varroa mites. Feeders provide supplemental nectar or sugar syrup when natural forage is scarce. Pollen patties can substitute for lack of pollen diversity. Having these extras before you get started with bees will prove handy.

When the hive becomes well established and produces surplus honey, you'll need some specialized gear for harvesting. A honey extractor spins frames to sling honey out of comb by centrifugal force. Extractors range from hand-cranked to electric and radial or tangential designs. Match your choice to the number of frames and hives you'll be harvesting. Uncapping forks slice wax caps off full frames prior to extracting. Hot knives quickly uncap as well. Uncapping tanks hold loose wax cappings after slinging. Filtering equipment removes wax and other debris from extracted honey. Food-grade buckets, jars, and bottles will be needed for bottling the harvest. With this equipment, you can reap and prepare your liquid gold reward.

Some additional supplies also make general hive management smoother for beekeepers. Keeping a hive logbook is crucial for recording observations and tasks performed during inspections. A soft bee brush gently moves bees when needed. Lit smokers, hive tools and other metals can be carried in a steel pail. A utility knife quickly opens sealed hive boxes. Leather gloves offer wrist protection when pulling sticky frames. Medications and hive treatments require proper storage away from sunlight. Having a ready supply of drawn comb frames or foundation helps with swarm control. Maintaining a full range of equipment enhances self-sufficiency in beekeeping.

There are a few other optional gadgets beekeepers may find helpful. Queen excluders are slotted metal or plastic sheets that allow worker bees through, while restricting the queen within a designated box. This helps control brood rearing locations. Escape boards provide a one-way exit to gently clear bees from honey supers. Parasitic mite screens monitor and manage hive pests. Pollen traps collect bee-collected pollen pellets at the entrance. Solar wax melters process wax cappings and old comb. Autoclave equipment sterilizes hive tools and components. While not strictly necessary, such specialty tools provide extra capabilities for those interested.

In summary, equipping yourself thoroughly before acquiring bees will give your apiary endeavors the best chance of success. Protective apparel, hive components, frame handling tools, maintenance supplies, and harvesting equipment comprise the essentials needed. While an investment, quality beekeeping gear enables you to create ideal living conditions for your colony. Assembling equipment aligned to your goals and budget lays the physical foundation. Beyond the physical tools though, continuing education provides the insights needed to use equipment skillfully. With both knowledge and equipment, you'll be ready to establish bees and put your beekeeping supplies to work.

Choosing Your Bee Breed

Selecting an appropriate honey bee breed is one of the most important decisions a beekeeper makes. The bee breed determines traits like disease resistance, productivity, and temperament that significantly influence colony success. While the majority of managed bees are of the Apis mellifera species, there are over 20 recognized subspecies or "races". Each race exhibits strengths and weaknesses based on their evolutionary adaptations. Key aspects to consider when choosing a bee breed include survivability in your climate, honey yield, disease/pest resistance, and temperament.

Climate matching enhances winter survival rates and year-round colony health. In temperate climates, hardy northern European breeds like the Carniolan and Italian bee thrive. The Carniolan originates from colder Alpine regions, so they rapidly build up honey stores in spring and tightly regulate brood rearing. This winter preparation and frugal brood rearing helps their winter hardiness. Their dark color also enables heating and foraging in cool temps. The Italian bee instead originated in the mild Mediterranean. Their extensive brood rearing can allow rapid spring build-up and high honey yields during prolonged warm seasons. But their lighter color and more open nesting make them vulnerable in extreme cold.

In southern warmer climates, breeds like the Buckfast and Africanized bee better tolerate heat and drought. The Africanized bee derives from the original tropical African subspecies. They are extremely defensive but have adapted to sustain brood rearing during periods of resource scarcity. The Buckfast bee was bred for traits like vigor and disease resistance to thrive in diverse European climates. Their mixed lineage provides adaptable, productive colonies across varying conditions. Matching your bees' native climate helps optimize seasonal survival and year-round strength.

Honey production is another distinguishing breed trait. In general, the Italian bee has long been favored for their ample honey yields. Their rapid spring build-up allows maximum foraging and storage space just when nectar flows peak. They exhibit excellent comb building to accommodate this honey. The Caucasian bee also produces copious honey with their large colony sizes and longer worker lifespans enabling more foraging days. In contrast, the Russian and Carniolan bees have a measured brood-rearing strategy more focused on winter survival than maximal summer honey production. The key is aligning preferred honey harvest levels with suitable breed productivity tendencies.

Disease and pest resistance should guide breed selection for colony health. The Varroa mite poses a major threat, transmitting viruses and sapping bee strength. Russian and Varroa-sensitive hygienic Italian strains specifically groom mites from brood cells. The Minnesota Hygienic line detects and removes infected pupae. These hygienic behaviors limit mite infestations without chemical treatment. Meanwhile, the Africanized bee coevolved with various tropical diseases and pests, conferring strong innate immunity. Prioritizing breeds with genetic disease defenses reduces reliance on medications.

Temperament is another pivotal consideration. Gentle bees enable relaxed hive inspections and safe honey harvesting. The Italian bee earns its popularity partially through their easy-going nature. The Carniolan similarly displays a gentle temperament that makes them a great choice for beginners. In contrast, the Caucasian and Africanized bee have more defensive tendencies, requiring great care and protective gear. Strains bred from the aggressive African bee are typically avoided by hobbyists. Keeping naturally gentle bees facilitates positive beekeeping experiences.

Ultimately local availability limits options for beekeepers in many regions. Finding regional bee suppliers is key to accessing well-adapted stock. In the Americas, most commercially available bees are Italian/Carniolan hybrids that blend common desirable traits. These "mutt" bees generate vigorous hybrid vigor. Seeking out local stocks also provides bees pre-acclimatized to prevailing conditions. Joining area associations connects you with nearby queen breeders. If importing bees from distant stocks, gradually transitioning to regional strains through requeening improves climatic suitability over time.

While most beginning beekeepers purchase pre-established hives, some opt to start from packaged bees. Key considerations for installing packaged bees include:

- Shake packages without the queen gently into the hive through the entrance.
- Carefully place the caged queen inside the hive.
- Feed the bees sugar syrup for the first weeks until incoming nectar flows strengthen.
- Monitor food levels and be prepared to continue feeding if inadequate natural forage is available.

- Leave the colony undisturbed for at least a week to allow bees to settle into their new home.
- Check after a week for eggs and larvae indicating the queen is laying.

Starting a hive from a package requires diligent initial care giving but allows selection of ideal breed traits. Shake packages are also cheaper than ready-built colonies. Just be sure to provide essential provisions while the bees establish themselves.

In summary, breed selection significantly influences colony productivity, health, and temperament. Match the breed to your climate, apicultural goals, and management preference. Seek out regional stocks and queen breeders for locally adapted bees. Thoroughly researching breed traits and consulting other beekeepers informs the critical choice of which bee is the best fit. Providing your bees with the conditions their particular genetics are evolved for sets up your colony for success.

Suiting Up for Safety

Beekeeping requires appropriate protective equipment to keep you safe when working your hives. While honey bees are generally docile, they will sting to defend their colony, so suiting up properly is an essential part of responsible apiary management.

The foundation of your beekeeping outfit begins with a hooded suit or jacket. It should be made of tightly-woven fabric to prevent bees from stinging through it. Light colors are preferable to avoid aggravating bees on hot days. The suit should include long sleeves with fitted cuffs and pant legs that close snugly around boots or shoes. Elastic hoods offer the best protection. You'll also need beekeeping gloves. Options like goatskin leather provide sting protection with dexterity for hive manipulations. Gauntlet-style gloves overlapping your sleeve cuffs help prevent gaps where bees can sneak in.

You have a few options when it comes to head and face shields. Many jackets have built-in wire mesh veils. For maximum visibility, a rounded hat with a see-through soft mesh veil is recommended. Some beekeepers use square veils that collapse into a easier-to-carry bundle when not worn. Helmets made of hard plastic offer robust facial defense as well. You may want to experiment with veil and helmet styles before investing in your preferred option. The veil or helmet should be securely attached to your suit or jacket.

Hard hats provide impact protection from hive parts or heavy smoke canisters. They are especially useful when working hives located overhead, like on steep slopes or rooftops. Cycling helmets and pith safari hats also adapt well to supplement bee suits. Base your headgear selection on your specific apiary environment.

For footwear, select leather boots at least knee-high with non-slip soles. Tuck your pants inside tightly to prevent bees climbing up your legs. You can also apply duct tape seals. Alternatively, full-body bee coveralls offer the most comprehensive protection. Pay special attention to sealing any suit openings prone to letting in bees, like neck closures or zippers.

Some additional equipment can further fortify your beekeeping attire:

- Beekeeping gloves with elongated sleeves to cover wrists and forearms
- Ankle gaiters that tie under footwear to close gaps at shoes
- Elastic bands at sleeve ends to constrict openings
- Tape around cuffs, ankles, and other access points
- A bee brush to gently remove bees from your suit

Proper dressing also makes working with bees more comfortable on hot days. Seek lightweight, breathable fabrics, especially in veils. Vents can be added to suits to improve ventilation. Some beekeepers don light colors to reflect heat. You may need to experiment with different materials and styles to find the ideal protective wear for your climate.

For smokers used to calm bees, select protective gloves resistant to burns. Fire retardant fabrics are sensible when using smoke around hives. Carry water or a fire extinguisher when working with smokers. Avoid loose clothing or dangling suit parts that could catch embers. Prevent tripping hazards from smoker fuel cans and accessories too.

The best way to test your beekeeping attire is to observe a hive, immersing yourself in the presence of bees. Gauge their reactions and watch for any areas they cluster or attempt to enter your gear. Adjust your suit accordingly to improve the seal at those points. You can also enlist a mentor to evaluate your outfit for gaps while you stand near an active hive. Taking these proactive measures will help identify flaws before you start handling frames and bees.

With the right protective ensemble expertly fitted, you can inspect hives with confidence. No wardrobe absolutely prevents stings, but conscientious precautions will enable you to manage hives effectively. Taking the time to suit up correctly demonstrates respect for the bees you keep. As you gain experience, you may even find some tasks can be carefully executed with minimal gear once you have a high comfort level. But default to wearing the full recommended attire when starting out and whenever attempting substantial hive work. Your dedication to safety will make beekeeping more enjoyable while also setting a prudent example for others.

Understanding Beekeeping Laws and Regulations

Beekeeping is a regulated activity in many areas, with laws and ordinances governing key aspects of hive management. It is the obligation of beekeepers to understand their legal responsibilities and adherence requirements. Regulations aim to support peaceful coexistence between beekeepers and their non-beekeeping neighbors. Most laws address permitting, hive placement, and required practices to control issues like swarming and colony defensiveness. Failure to comply with beekeeping laws can result in fines, hive confiscation or loss of permits.

A first step for aspiring beekeepers is to check local ordinances for any permitting requirements. Many urban and suburban municipalities require hobbyist beekeepers to formally register their hives. Permits help ensure beekeepers are educated on proper management techniques. Annual permit fees offset administrative expenses like maintaining a beekeeper registry and responding to public questions or complaints. Renewing a permit requires proof that education requirements were met each year. Failing to obtain a permit where mandated can lead to legal repercussions.

Researching laws helps identify optimal hive placement to avoid conflicts. Hives must be situated with appropriate setbacks from property lines and common areas. Urban beekeeping ordinances provide specific setback distances, often 10-25 feet from adjacent lots. This prevents crossing property lines during foraging. Setbacks from public spaces like sidewalks, parks and community gardens are larger, typically 25-50 feet. These aim to limit pedestrian exposure. Rules also commonly specify hives cannot be located in front yards visible from the street. Backyard or screened side yard placement maintains discretion.

Most localities also limit the number of hives allowed per property. In dense neighborhoods, permitting may restrict residents to 2-4 hives. More permissive rural areas often allow 6-10 hives without a special use permit. These caps aim to prevent extremely large apiaries in residential zones. They also reduce nuisance complaints by curtailing excessive hive activity and bee traffic in densely populated blocks. Understanding number limits enables proper apiary scaling.

Beekeepers must follow mandates on providing fresh water sources. Bees will seek water from neighborhood swimming pools, bird baths and other sources if not provided on-site. Ordinances therefore require beekeepers to supply clean water with features like floats or ramps to prevent drowning. Installing water early in the season prevents bees from establishing off-site water collection habits.

Several practices are legally mandated to control defensive behavior issues. Requeening colonies displaying aggressive tendencies is required to restore docility. Hives must be gently handled to prevent provoking attacks. Smokers should be used when inspecting hives to disguise alarm pheromones. Situating hive openings away from active areas minimizes defensive responses to disturbances. These measures aim to prevent aggressive incidents involving pets, pedestrians or neighbors.

Regulations also target issues like swarming, colony hygiene and pest control. To prevent swarming, beekeepers must provide adequate living space and split overcrowded hives. Capturing and rehousing swarms that do escape is mandated. Maintaining cleanliness in the hive and surroundings reduces disease risk. Monitoring for pests and promptly addressing infestations protects colony health. Neglecting these legally enforceable measures can compromise hives and nearby properties.

Compliance enables positive community relations and ongoing beekeeping privileges. Many ordinances include provisions to revoke permits following multiple valid complaints or violations. Hive confiscation, fines or criminal citations can result from disregarding regulations. Joining a local beekeepers association provides education on regional laws and avoidance tips. Being proactive with required practices also reduces neighbor issues. Overall knowledge of and compliance with laws safeguards happy hives.

Understanding regulations protects beekeepers from legal liabilities as well. Hives must be managed in ways that reasonably prevent injury incidents. Homeowner's insurance should specifically cover beekeeping activities. Not adhering to defensive bee mandates could invalidate policies following incidents. Product liability insurance helps hedge against issues from selling hive products. Staying informed on laws and insurance requirements makes beekeeping a risk-aware pursuit.

Advocating for positive policy changes is another civic engagement avenue. Outdated bans on urban beekeeping are being repealed across many communities to support sustainable local agriculture. Modern ordinances with education requirements enable responsible urban pollination. Active local beekeeper groups often lobby for bee-friendly reforms. Laws should strike a balance between enabling safe beekeeping and protecting community interests.

In summary, a working knowledge of regional beekeeping laws allows you to manage hives in compliance from the start. Follow permitting procedures where required. Abide by setbacks and colony number limits in siting hives. Provide fresh water sources on-site. Employ techniques to limit swarming and aggression. Maintain clean hives and healthy bees. Insurance coverage tailored for beekeeping offers protection. And considering ways to support constructive regulations preserves beekeepers' privileges while protecting communities. Keeping harmony with neighbors and the law makes the sweetness of beekeeping possible.

CHAPTER 3

BUILDING YOUR FIRST HIVE

Choosing the Right Location

Selecting an appropriate apiary site is one of the most important decisions a beekeeper makes. The location of your hives will impact the health and productivity of your bees. When scouting potential spots, look for these ideal conditions:

Access to ample floral sources is vital. Bees forage within a 2-3 mile radius, so hives should be situated near diverse, bee-friendly vegetation. A mix of wildflowers, trees, bushes, gardens, and orchards will provide nectar and pollen from spring through fall. native plants suited to your region are ideal. Rural pastures, meadows, forest edges, and roadside vegetation offer seasonal variety. In urban areas, community gardens and landscaping can supplement forage. Avoid fields treated with pesticides. Also check that sufficient clean water sources exist nearby.

Choose a sunny, south-facing position sheltered from wind. Bees rely on sunshine and require temperatures above 50°F to fly out and forage. Hives should receive at least 6 hours of direct sun, free from shade. Orient hive entrances away from prevailing winds to prevent chilling and make take-offs and landings easier. Natural windbreaks like fences, hedges, or structures can help block gusts.

If possible, place hives on a gentle slope to enhance drainage during wet weather. This prevents waterlogging that stresses colonies. Elevating hives on platforms in flood-prone areas also safeguards from rising water. In arid climates, be mindful not to site hives where they will overheat on scorching summer days. Optimal hive temperature ranges from around 92-95°F.

It's preferable to locate hives off the ground to deter pests. Elevated stands deter skunks, mice, and hive beetles from accessing hives. Raising colonies also makes inspections easier on your back. Aim for waist-to-shoulder height. You can construct basic hive stands using concrete blocks, pallets, or other materials. Strap hives securely to prevent toppling in winds.

For convenience, hives should be reasonably accessible by vehicle or foot while working. However, keep hives discreetly sited away from high-traffic areas. Bee activity can disturb neighbors or public spaces. Avoid children's play areas, sidewalks, and other high-density locations. Post warning signs if needed. Also consider proximity to your home - flights paths shouldn't direct bees toward doors, pools, or patios.

When siting multiple hives, allow adequate spacing between colonies. As a general rule, permit at least 6-10 feet between hives, with more distance preferred. This prevents overcrowding and drifting between colonies. It also reduces opportunities for diseases and parasites to spread from one hive to another.

You must comply with local zoning laws and homeowner association rules when selecting an apiary site. Some municipalities impose licensing or restrictions on beekeeping, especially in residential areas. Maintain positive community relations by staying discreet. Privacy fences, hedges, and other barriers help conceal hives.

No location is perfect. WHEN COMPROMISES ARE NEEDED, RELIABLE FORAGE SOURCES AND SHELTER FROM ELEMENTS SHOULD TAKE PRIORITY. Minor drawbacks like distance from home or sloped terrain can be overcome. But no amount of convenience outweighs starving, weather-stressed bees. Take a holistic perspective when evaluating potential spots.

In summary, base your apiary placement on these priorities:

- Abundant forage plants and water within flight range

- Maximize sun exposure and protection from winds

- Gentle slope for drainage, elevated above ground

- Reasonably accessible for hive management

- Follow zoning laws and community etiquette

- Allow adequate spacing between multiple hives

With a knowledge of your region's climate and landscape, you can select ideal hive positions tailored to your bees' needs. Monitor colony performance at any prospective apiary locations through the seasons. Be prepared to move hives if poor productivity, pest issues, or other limitations arise. Your final choice should set your new beekeeping venture up for success.

Types of Beehives

Several fundamental styles of beehives exist, each with distinct advantages and disadvantages. The type of hive impacts space allocation, access for inspections, honey harvesting ease, and more. Key factors in selecting a hive type include the size and number of desired colonies, convenience of use for the beekeeper, intended honey production levels, and overwintering in colder climates. Beginning hobbyists typically choose between basic Langstroth and top bar hives. Understanding the core options helps match the hive to both bees' and keeper's needs.

The Langstroth hive is the most ubiquitous style in beekeeping today. Reverend Lorenzo Langstroth patented this movable frame hive in 1853. Its enduring popularity stems from several key innovations. Langstroth hives contain vertical frames that hang within the box, separated by bee space. This critical gap of 1/4 to 3/8 inches lets bees move freely over both sides of each frame. The movable frames permit easy hive inspections and honey harvesting without dismantling comb. Langstroth's clever dimensional design based on bee space maximizes usable space while minimizing burr comb between frames.

Today's Langstroth hives contain stacked, modular boxes called supers. A brood box on bottom contains the queen and brood comb. Supers added above provide space for honey storage and additional brood rearing. Standard 10-frame Langstroth supers keep colonies moderately sized. Alternatives like 8-frame boxes offer more limited space for smaller yields. Many parts like woodenware boxes, frames, covers and bottoms are interchangeable between manufacturers. This versatility and standardization makes Langstroth hives ideal for both hobbyists and commercial operators.

Top bar hives provide a lower-cost, lower-maintenance alternative well-suited to small-scale beekeeping. These single-chamber hives contain elongated top bars that allow bees to build vertical comb beneath without a supporting frame. The lack of frames means less equipment to purchase upfront. It also provides bees more freedom to build natural, varied comb sizes. Horizontal orientation of combs enables easier inspections without heavy lifting. But honey harvesting requires actually cutting comb off the bars, making the process more labor intensive.

Advantages of a top bar hive include smaller initial investment, simpler woodworking skills needed for construction, and a balance of natural comb that some believe is healthiest for bees. Their limitations come in terms of honey production and wintering ability. A single chamber offers much less honey storage than stacked Langstroth boxes. The large combs with honey storage directly above brood rearing areas also makes winter preparation challenging for bees. But for hobbyists seeking moderate honey for personal use, top bar hives offer an appealing option.

Warré hives offer an alternative vertical stacking hive that shares some benefits of top bar hives. It also contains modular boxes, but instead of movable frames, bees build fixed comb onto starter strips on the box walls. This freestanding comb enables natural cell size and bee space between combs. Access is through the top, with boxes added to the bottom as the colony expands downward. Warré hives thus have reduced disruption compared to the Langstroth system. They can also be top-bar converted for ease of comb removal. The downsides are very limited inspections and the need to destroy comb to harvest honey. But those seeking a "bee-centric" approach favor Warré hives for aligning more closely with natural nesting behaviors.

Alternative hive styles enable unique benefits but come with limitations around productivity and management. Hive choice depends partly on climate conditions. Top bar and Warré hives often prove challenging where winters are long and cold. Their single-cavity design makes it difficult for bees to effectively utilize stored food or generate heat through the winter. Langstroth hives with concentrated honey stores immediately above the brood nest overwinter most successfully in harsher climates.

Maximizing honey production also favors Langstroth hives. The stacked boxes with movable frames allow generating much larger bee populations and honey stores. Top bar and Warré hives yield enough honey for personal use but are impractical for larger-scale production. Langstroth hives additionally make inspecting, breeding, splitting, and pest control activities easier for beekeepers to perform. For those interested purely in pollination rather than honey, the more "hands-off" top bar and Warré hives allow bees greater self-determination.

Other niche hive styles also exist, like AZ and Kenyan top bar hives. But Langstroth, top bar, and Warré hives constitute the primary options with notable uptake. Understanding the core differences enables matching a hive type to your climate, space constraints, beekeeping goals, budget and philosophical approach. There is no universally "best" option. With research and planning, choosing a well-suited hive style sets up bees and keepers for mutual success.

Constructing Your Hive

Building your own beehives allows customization and can save costs compared to purchasing pre-made equipment. With basic carpentry skills and the right materials, you can construct complete hive setups tailored to your operation.

You'll need untreated lumber, ideally pine or cedar which resist decay. Standard dimensions are:

- Boxes - 19 7/8" x 16 1/4" x 9 5/8"
- Frames - 16 1/4" x 9 1/4"
- Bottoms - 48" x 16 1/4" with entrance reducer
- Covers - 48" x 16 1/4" with overhang
- Other materials: nails, screws, wood glue, paint

The brood box is the primary hive component, holding 8-10 frames where bees raise young and store honey. A "deep" sized box is recommended, providing ample space as colonies grow. Construct boxes with lap joints at the corners for sturdiness. Include handholds for easy lifting. Waterproof glue and nail or screw boxes together.

Frames give bees comb foundation to build on within the boxes. Top bars should measure 1 1/4". Cut side bars, notch them to hold top bars, and assemble into rectangles. Install wax or plastic sheeting into the frames for bees to draw out comb. Staple in place and embed in wax.

The hive bottom supports the stack. Use a wide board or plywood fitted with a sliding entrance reducer. This controls ventilation and access. Screened bottom boards can deter pests while enhancing ventilation. Leaving the bottom board open mesh aids in monitoring hive health. Solid bottoms with small entrances also work well.

Telescoping hive covers protect the colony from weather. Use shiplap or board-and-batten construction to make removable, weatherproof lids with 2-3" overhangs. Insulate covers with rigid foam or burlap for temperature moderation. Apply waterproof sealant or paint to the outside.

Ventilating boxes called honey supers give bees space to store surplus honey, placed above the brood chamber. Medium supers are recommended for versatility. Add more supers as the hive expands. Include an entrance notch so bees can access the honey storage.

Essential accessories include a entrance feeder, smoker for hive calming, and hive tool. Create a peaked metal roof or shingles to shield hive tops. Elevate hives on stands or concrete blocks to deter pests.

Paint hive exteriors with primer and two coats of exterior latex paint for weather protection. Neutral colors like white, beige or green are ideal. Avoid dark hues that may overheat bees. Brand your equipment for identification and deter theft.

Adhere to specific construction techniques for best results:

- Precision cuts and seamless joins
- Water-resistant wood glue for bonds
- Galvanized nails and exterior-grade screws
- Pre-drill holes to prevent wood splitting
- Sand parts smooth to limit propolis build-up
- Use food-safe, non-toxic paints only

Follow exact measurements for hive components to ensure proper bee space between frames. This spacing is key to preventing burr comb and overcrowding issues.

Building your own equipment requires some woodworking skill and proper safety precautions. But the ability to customize hive dimensions and styles to suit your needs makes it a worthwhile investment. Your homemade hives will provide functional, cost-effective housing tailored for your bees' success.

In summary, construct Langstroth hives using:

- Deep brood boxes with 8-10 frames
- Telescoping covers with insulation and overhangs
- Matching honey supers for additional storage
- Sturdy screened bottom boards with entrances
- Accessories like feeders, smokers, tools
- Stands or blocks to elevate hives
- Prime and paint exteriors for weather protection

With drafted plans, quality materials, and carpentry finesse, you can assemble complete hive setups yourself. The hands-on process gives you creative control and pride of ownership. Your bees will thrive in homemade hives built with care to suit their essential needs.

Preparing Your Hive for Bees

Once you've acquired the necessary equipment, preparing the physical hive for installation of a new bee colony is the next key step. Proper initial setup creates ideal conditions for your bees to thrive.

Assembling the hive boxes and frames to house the colony comes first. For common Langstroth hives, stack a bottom brood chamber with a screened bottom board beneath it. Place an entrance reducer at the front opening. Install wax or plastic foundations into wooden frames, securing each with wire or plastic tabs. Load frames into the brood box, leaving an empty gap along each sidewall for mobility.

Above the brood chamber, add a queen excluder to separate it from honey supers. The excluder prevents the queen from moving up to lay eggs in honey frames reserved for harvest. Place an initial honey super filled with frames atop the excluder. Top the stack with the inner cover, applying a thin bead of vegetable shortening around the rim to block gaps. Telescoping top covers then enclose everything while allowing ventilation.

With the hive assembled, next comes properly siting it. Choose a flat, stable area partly shaded that allows morning sun and afternoon shade. Face the hive entrance away from harsh winds but with a flight path unobstructed by vegetation. Raise it a few inches on concrete blocks, stands or a pallet to deter moisture issues. Make sure to level the base; a bubble level is ideal to check plumb. Secure the hive against tipping over from animals. Discourage ants by keeping vegetation cleared away from hive legs.

For convenience, keep the hive within 50 yards of an accessible water source. Bees will frequent bird baths, fountains and livestock troughs. Ensure the hive is in a reasonably quiet spot distant from high traffic areas or noise pollution. Your goal is providing an appealing oasis where bees can productively forage and manufacture honey undisturbed.

Preparing for hive inspections and maintenance comes next. With the hive assembled and leveled, place an overturned empty super or follower board behind the last frame. This follower board will gently corral the colony within the cavity initially. Install an entrance cleat to pry the front open. Have your smoker filled, lit and ready for calming bees. Ensure hive tools and other gear is clean and on hand for immediate use.

When introducing the new colony, have extra equipment ready to expand the hive as the population grows. Place drawn comb, foundations, frames, supers, inner covers and lids nearby for seamless expansions. Nearby have a bucket of sugar syrup and pollen patties available to supplement natural foraging.

Monitoring and record keeping are also key. Establish a hive inspection schedule, starting with weekly or bi-weekly when a new colony is first introduced. Purchase a weatherproof hive logbook to detail observations and actions taken during checks. Writing on removable paper inserts allows summarizing notes later. Label each super and frame for tracking. Have a marker pen handy to document frame order and hive arrangements.

Understanding what to look for during early inspections will help you assess the hive's condition. Food stores should accumulate evenly on frames. Note any spotty brood pattern issues. Verify the queen is laying eggs and check for queen cells. Look for signs of diseases like chalkbrood mummies or parasites such as Varroa mites. Monitor bees' demeanor for indications of colony strength. Keep records to inform maintenance decisions and establish seasonal baselines unique to each hive.

Preparing yourself with the right protective gear is also essential before installing bees. Obtain a hooded bee suit or jacket with elastic cuffs and zippered veil. High-quality leather gloves in the appropriate sizing allow dexterity when manipulating frames. Choose gloves with extended wrists for ventilation and overlap with your sleeves. Have an extra pair of gloves on hand in case of stings through the first pair. Wear boots or closed-toe shoes with socks covering ankles completely. Bring a hat and veil for any observers present. With proper attire, stinging risk is greatly reduced when working with defensive bees.

Besides physical equipment, take time to educate yourself prior to acquiring your colony. Read manuals on beekeeping basics and join online forums to ask questions. Take a hands-on class to gain experience lighting smokers, opening hives and handling frames with instructor guidance. Understand your regional seasonal fluctuations, typical bloom periods, and foraging conditions. Research your legal obligations for registration, hive placement and pest management. Being as informed as possible before starting with bees will set you up for success.

In summary, laying the groundwork makes a difference in getting your first colony established. Assembling hive components properly, positioning the hive strategically, preparing hive tools and attire, and educating yourself on what to expect will ensure you and your bees transition smoothly into the new partnership ahead. With advance preparation, you can start managing your colony with greater skill, safety and confidence right away.

Introducing Bees to Your Hive

Installing a colony of bees is an exciting milestone in the beekeeping journey. Proper introduction sets up bees for success in their new home. Key elements include preparing the hive, acquiring bees, transporting them safely, installing the colony, and providing essential early care. Taking measures to support a smooth transition helps bees quickly settle into their new hive.

Before bees arrive, the hive must be fully assembled, cleaned, and readied with basic provisions. For Langstroth hives, this includes installing wax foundation into frames and arranging frames in the brood box. Ensure frames are pushed tightly together to prevent initial cross combing. Top bar hives require positioning bars evenly spaced across the top. In all hives, include oriented comb guides so bees build straight combs aligned for easy removal. Applying a coating of wax helps attract bees to start building on foundations.

Leaving some drawn comb from a previous colony helps bees immediately start brood rearing. Drawn comb also provides scent cues making the space feel established. Alternately shake in a package of bees to impart hive scent. Remove any debris like wood shavings or dead bees from boxes. Finally position the bottom board with entrance facing the anticipated flight path. Defining the "front" entrance early prevents comb misalignment. With the hive interior fully prepped, acquiring your bees is the next step.

Most hobbyists install packaged bees or retrieve swarms for their first colony. Packaged bees with a mated queen can be ordered from reputable suppliers in early spring. Request a package with feeding syrup and a marshmallow separating queen from workers for easy installation. Capturing a swarm from the wild enables free bees but requires skill identifying the queen. Another option is purchasing a nucleus colony with bees covering 2-5 frames along with a laying queen. Nucs with brood allow faster spring build-up.

When picking up packaged bees, avoid leaving them confined for long in hot conditions. Keep packages shaded with ventilation holes open. Misting the screen provides cooling and hydration. Never shake or sharply tilt packages to avoid harming the queen. Gently load and securely transport the package to prevent damaging movements enroute.

Upon arriving home, place the package in a cool, shaded spot and prepare the hive. Remove several outer frames to create an open space for releasing bees. Keep the colony entrance fully open for easy entry. Carefully pour bees from the package into the hive. Shake the remaining cluster directly in front of the entrance so they walk inside. Search for and gently place the caged queen within the brood nest.

Remove the queen cage candy plug after a few days so workers can slowly integrate her. Feeding the released bees 1:1 sugar syrup supports comb production. After several days quietly inspect to verify the queen was released and is laying eggs. Once the queen and majority of bees have relocated into the drawn combs, replace the empty frames to encourage further wax building.

With new swarms, first focus on carefully capturing the queen in a ventilated box. Then gently scoop and shake remaining bees directly into the prepared hive. Nucleus colonies can be transferred frame-by-frame into an established hive box. Position frames in the same order to keep brood nests undisturbed.

All newly housed bees require attentive care and minimal disturbance as they settle in. Continue feeding syrup until bees store excess honey. Monitor food levels to prevent starvation. Refill water sources frequently as activity increases. Ensure the hive has proper ventilation but is not drafty. Perform inspections gently after a week to check queen status. Resist opening the hive excessively to avoid disrupting wax production and the critical transition period.

With appropriate introduction techniques, bees generally adapt well to their new home. Signs of successful establishment include bees foraging from the hive, orienting flights, guard bees patrolling the entrance, and wax comb production. Brood rearing confirms the queen is mated and laying normally. Pollen collection indicates normal nutrition. Evidence of food storage shows bees are processing nectar flows. Normal hive activity signifies a smooth transition.

Troubleshooting issues arising during introduction helps get the colony firmly established:

- If the queen is lost or rejected, order an urgent queen replacement. Combine weak queenless bees with a stronger hive.

- Supplement feeding if poor weather limits natural forage. Support nutrition until flows strengthen.

- Cull any frames with cross-comb or burr comb and replace with fresh foundation. This prevents ongoing problems.

- Monitor for pests like ants or wax moths that could infiltrate the new colony.

- Ensure the hive remains fully ventilated to prevent excessive moisture or humidity.

- Consider using a hive entrance reducer to help bees defend against robbing by stronger hives.

Overall patience and support in the vulnerable introduction phase gives bees the conditions they need to accept their new home. Attentive monitoring ensures you catch any problems early before they escalate. Starting strong is the first step to honeybee health and satisfaction from your own apiary rewards.

CHAPTER 4

CARING FOR YOUR BEES

Monitoring Your Hive

Regular hive inspections are essential for monitoring your bees' health, spotting issues early, and gauging productivity.

Plan to inspect hives about once every 7-10 days during the active season. Check hives later in the day when most foragers are out. Avoid cold, wet, or windy conditions that stress bee colonies. Have your protective gear on and smoke generator ready before opening any hive. Apply smoke gently at the entrance and under the cover to calm bees before lifting the cover.

Scan the hive top and entrance first. Look for signs like dead bees, small hive beetles, ants, or wax cappings that provide clues about hive conditions. Remove the cover carefully to avoid crushing bees beneath it. Gently smoke the top bars of the uppermost box and wait a minute before proceeding. This gives the bees time to gorge on honey and remain peaceful.

Systematically lift each frame to assess its status. Track your inspection order to evenly distribute disruption. Gently brush bees off frames with a bee brush rather than shaking comb. Look for eggs and larvae of all stages, indicating a healthy, laying queen. Spot check brood cell cappings for uniformity - any perforations or inconsistencies warrant further examination.

Check both sides of every frame for indicators of colony health:

- Adequate food stores: at least 15+ lbs. surplus honey
- Pollen reserves: colorful, plentiful pollen bands

- Brood pattern: solid, compact areas of egg laying
- Pests: beetles, mites, ants, waxworms, etc.
- Diseases: chalkbrood, sacbrood, fungi
- Queen cells: preparation to swarm or supersede
- Crowding: need to add space

Make mental notes of your observations as you go, or use a hive inspection checklist. Track frames with eggs, capped brood, honey and pollen stores. Watch for evidence of queenlessness like spotty brood patterns. Signs of swarm preparations like overcrowding, queen cells, and backfilling brood require prompt action.

If the queen is sighted, check her health and egg laying status. Clip her wingtips to prevent swarming. Monitor food reserves and add supplements if inadequate. Install queen excluders if needed for honey harvesting. Equalize frame distribution across boxes if necessary.

Always carefully reassemble the hive, replacing frames in the same configuration. Never leave comb exposed for long, as chilling brood can be fatal. Replenish smoke if bees become agitated during inspection. Go slowly and gently to prevent provoking defensive behaviors.

Keeping detailed inspection records allows you to compare observations and trends over time. Note the quantity of bees, brood, food storage, and other metrics each visit. Track dates of hive manipulations, mite treatments, and supplemental feeding for reference. Records help optimize hive management.

Try to disturb the bees as little possible during inspections. Limit your visit to under 10 minutes in summer or 5 minutes during colder months when bee movement is sluggish. Close up the hive smoothly and allow the colony to settle before you leave the area.

In summary, monitor hives by:

- Inspecting every 7-10 days at calm times
- Checking for disease, pests, food reserves, and other health indicators
- Carefully examining each frame systematically
- Assessing brood pattern, queen status, and other key factors
- Taking detailed notes on observations and comparisons
- Minimizing disruption time and keeping the hive stable

With regular, low-stress hive observations, you can stay apprised of your bees' changing conditions throughout seasons. Diligent monitoring allows you to maintain strong, productive colonies by addressing any deficiencies or threats before they escalate.

Feeding Your Bees

Providing proper nutrition is crucial for maintaining strong honey bee colonies. As a beekeeper, you may need to supplement your bees' diet with an artificial food source when their honey stores run low or floral resources are scarce. Feeding bees both replaces depleted reserves and stimulates colony growth.

When first establishing hives, begin by feeding bees a 1:1 sugar water solution. Mix one part white granulated sugar with one part hot water by volume. Avoid other sugar types. The water should be warm to fully dissolve the sugar when mixing the syrup. Allow it to fully cool before feeding it to bees to prevent overheating them. Never give bees plain water, which can drown them.

Feed this sugar syrup directly into empty comb using tools like Boardman feeders, hive-top feeders, or baggies with holes poked in them. Start with a thin syrup mixture to mimic nectar. Gradually thicken the consistency up to a 2:1 ratio as the bees store away reserves for winter. Feed until at least two full combs contain capped sugar syrup, providing 15-20 pounds of stored food.

Pollen substitute patties can also boost protein intake, supporting brood rearing and colony growth. Commercially available substitutes contain pollen, soy flour, brewer's yeast, milk powder and essential oils. Place small patties on the top bars of brood frames, replacing every few weeks as they get consumed.

Always monitor food levels when inspecting hives. During times of natural nectar dearth, continue supplementary feeding to prevent starvation. Feed again in late fall to provide vital winter food stores. Aim to have 60-80 pounds of honey stored in the hive by winter.

In spring, resume feeding thin sugar syrup to energize growth and comb production. As natural nectar flows resume, taper off artificial feeding to avoid filling combs with winter-prone syrup. Target feeds to stimulate wax building, not simply replacing honey consumed.

Take care not to spill syrups and attract pests. Use hive feeders designed for clean, protected feeding. Replenish syrup as needed but don't allow it to stagnate and spoil. Keep records of feeding times and quantities provided to each hive.

When feeding, some key guidelines include:

- Mix hot syrup and allow it to fully cool before use
- Start with 1:1 syrup, gradually thickening to 2:1 ratio
- Target feeds during establishment, dearths, and pre-winter
- Avoid spillage and use hive-mounted feeders
- Give protein patties to support brood production
- Taper off feeding as seasonal nectar flows resume
- Ensure adequate winter stores of 60-80 pounds

With close monitoring and properly timed feeding, you can optimize nutrition intake. Research shows well-nourished colonies experience improved health, longevity and honey production.

Yet improper feeding carries risks. Overfeeding syrup can inhibit natural foraging and lead to unhealthy diets. Excess midseason feeds may also promote swarming or cause bees to pack supplies into brood chambers. Familiarize yourself with the seasonal, supplemental nutrition needs of your specific apiary.

In summary, key feeding goals include:

- Establishing new hives with syrup and patties
- Sustaining colonies during dearth periods
- Maximizing winter food reserves
- Energizing spring build-up and comb production
- Supporting brood-rearing with protein supplements
- Preventing starvation and promoting colony health

With a fundamental understanding of honey bee nutrition and a feeding regimen tailored to your climate, you can ensure your bees get the sustenance they require to thrive all year long.

Managing Pests and Diseases

One key responsibility of beekeepers is monitoring for and controlling hive pests and diseases. Left unchecked, common pathogens and invaders can weaken and devastate honey bee colonies. Strategic integrated pest management enables bees to thrive in managed hives.

Varroa mites are currently the most destructive parasite facing honey bees globally. Varroa feed on bee hemolymph, acting as disease vectors for virulent viruses. Reproduction happens within capped brood cells. Rapid mite population growth coupled with associated viral infections can lead to colony collapse. Monitoring through sticky boards, ether rolls, and visual examination is critical. Timely miticide treatments using thymol, formic acid, oxalic acid and Apiguard maintain safe mite levels. Non-chemical controls like drone brood trapping and powdered sugar shakes also help suppress mites. Requeening with mite-resistant stock improves tolerance.

Nosema is a fungal gut pathogen that causes dysentery and reduces productivity and lifespan. Bees appear sluggish and hive populations dwindle. Microscope spore analysis of bee bread or bee guts diagnoses nosema type and load. Fumagillin is the only approved treatment, applied either spring/fall preventively or in early infection. Good nutrition and reducing stress helps strengthen bees against nosema. Replace comb and thoroughly disinfect hives annually to prevent spore buildup.

Chalkbrood results from another fungal pathogen, Ascosphaera apis, that mummifies larvae. Hard chalky-white larvae dotting comb signals infection. Providing good ventilation and nutrition minimizes outbreak severity. Requeen to introduce genetic hygienic behavior. Bacillus thuringiensis (BT) has shown some effectiveness. Remove and destroy severely infested frames.

American and European Foulbrood are highly contagious, antibiotic-resistant bacterial diseases. Rows of sunken, discolored punctured brood cells indicate infection. Laboratory analysis differentiates between the two types. Most states mandate burning severely infected hives to contain spread. Oxytetracycline or tylosin treatments during light infection may be effective, but requeening is recommended. Maintain strict sanitation and replace old comb regularly as prevention.

Small hive beetles are a destructive scavenger pest. Larvae tunnel through comb to eat honey, ruin wax, and cause fermentation and honey slime. Adults congregate in clusters. Monitor with in-hive traps. Keep populations down through net screenings, drone comb traps, and insecticides. Maintain strong hives; weak colonies are more susceptible. Remove and cull infested comb promptly before damage spreads.

Wax moths similarly tunnel through frames as larvae, webbing and destroying comb. Adults lay eggs in unattended supers and stored frames. Regular strong hives control them through hive hygiene. Stacked, unused boxes should be stored in airtight containers. Moth traps draw adults for monitoring and removal. Freezing or fumigating comb kills all life stages. Keeping drawn comb to a minimum avoids problems. Discard damaged comb immediately.

Robbing by other bees or insects threatens weak or disrupted hives suddenly overloaded with unguarded honey. Block the entrance except for a small opening bees can defend. Move hives away from high traffic areas if needed. Reduce entrances at night when robbing often occurs. Equalize colonies by adding or removing resources cautiously. Repair any hive damage promptly.

Prevention is the first line of defense against viruses like Deformed Wing Virus. Maintain low mite levels, replace queens, and minimize mixing hives during infection periods. No direct treatments exist, but good nutrition and reducing stressors boosts colony immunity. Cull drone brood from infected hives to limit spread through mating.

With vigilance and prompt action, most pest and disease issues can be managed at non-lethal levels. Monitoring through regular hive inspections allows early problem detection. Isolate and treat infected hives. Sterilize equipment between hives to restrict spread. Rotate out old brood comb and

Bee Health and Colony Collapse Disorder

Ensuring honey bee health is an essential responsibility for beekeepers. Bees face myriad threats from pests, diseases, pesticides, and poor nutrition. Colony collapse disorder (CCD) poses a particular risk, causing the rapid, unexplained disappearance of seemingly strong colonies. Understanding common health issues and implementing integrated pest management enables prevention and prompt treatment when problems arise.

Varroa mites are currently the most destructive threat to bee health. Varroa feed on bee larvae and adults, transmitting deadly viruses and suppressing immunity. Mites proliferate exponentially in a hive, quickly sickening and killing colonies without intervention. Monitoring mite levels through sticky boards or alcohol washes enables early detection. Integrated pest management combines screened bottom boards, drone brood removal, and approved miticides to control infestations. Timely mite treatment is imperative for colony survival.

Nosema is a fungal gut parasite that also weakens and shortens the lives of bees. Spores spread via contaminated comb, food, and feces. Dysentery, early supersedure, and colony decline can result from high Nosema levels. Microscope examination of bee abdomens identifies infection. Preventive measures include sterilizing comb and equipment between seasons, isolating sick colonies, and prompt treatment with approved antifungals.

Viruses transmitted by Varroa mites present another biological hazard. Deformed wing virus (DWV) causes shriveled wings, shortened abdomens, paralysis, and death. Sacbrood also leads to larval death, creating a gondola-shaped "melted" appearance. Regular mite control limits viral spread. Culling bees with severe symptoms prevents proliferation. Viral impacts can be mitigated but not cured.

Nutritional stress makes bees more vulnerable to health issues. Poor nutrition impairs metabolism, immunity, and overall vigor. Lack of pollen diversity prevents adequate protein intake. Insufficient honey stores lead to starvation. Providing supplemental feeding sustains bees during periods of dearth. Testing pollen in wax comb or patty supplements indicates nutritional gaps to be addressed. Robust nutrition underpins bee health.

Pesticides also threaten honey bee fitness. Chemical residues accumulate in wax, pollen, and honey, creating chronic toxicity. Acute exposure can kill forager bees and larvae. Sublethal effects include neurological disruption, reduced egg laying, and impaired homing ability. Using integrated pest management, seeking out pesticide-free forage, and advocating for bee-safe regulations can reduce these dangers. Avoiding chemical controls within the hive is also vital.

Destructive hive beetles and wax moths take advantage of weakened colonies. Beetles consume pollen, honey and brood. Larvae tunnel through comb. Strong hives can corral and eject invaders, but stressed hives can quickly collapse from infestations. Monitoring for early signs like frass and cocoons allows quick responses like traps, insecticides, or comb freezing before extensive damage occurs. Maintaining robust bee health is key to preventing takeover.

Good general husbandry practices promote longevity and immunity. Requeening with young prolific queens boosts egg laying. Providing adequate living space reduces overcrowding pathogens. Eliminating burr comb deprives pests of 藏 sites. Exchanging old brood comb removes potential contaminants. Equalizing hive strength across the apiary limits robbing stress. Protecting colonies from excessive heat, cold, wind, and moisture reduces environmental stressors. Prevention is truly the best medicine for bees.

Colony collapse disorder poses a unique challenge, causing large proportions of workers to rapidly vanish from hives. Adult bees simply disappear without dead bodies remaining behind. Collapses leave empty hives with capped brood, food stores, and a few nurse bees who then perish. There are multiple hypothesized contributors to CCD including cumulative pesticide toxicity, pathogens, malnutrition, and climate stress. Complex interactions between these factors cause sudden, unrecoverable colony failure.

Strategies to reduce CCD losses center on building general colony health and immunity. Providing sufficient natural forage and biodiverse nutrition supports overall vigor. Integrated pest management helps control parasite and disease pressures. Limiting pesticide exposure through hive placement and advocacy protects bees from toxins. Careful tracking of stores ensures adequate year-round food reserves. Maintaining hives with proper space, ventilation, sunlight access, and protection from weather extremes reduces environmental stressors. Requeening with resistant stock improves genetics over time. While definitive solutions remain elusive, proactive health management gives bees their best chance against CCD.

In summary, honey bees face diverse menaces from pests, diseases, toxins, malnutrition, and mysterious CCD impacts. Staying vigilant for signs of declining health allows early intervention. Mite monitoring, disease screening, pathogen control, nutritional supplementation, sanitation methods, resistance breeding, and minimizing toxins are key prevention practices. Strong colonies better withstand inevitable pressures. Supporting bee health yields productive hives, reduces losses, and fulfils ethical obligations to our vital pollinators. With attentive care, hardy bees continue providing ecological services essential to ecosystems and agriculture.

Winterizing Your Hive

Preparing your hives for winter is essential to ensure your bees survive the colder months. Adequate food stores, protection from the elements, and preventative health measures will give your colony the best chance of emerging strong in spring.

Start preparations in late summer by determining if colonies have adequate honey reserves. Shoot for 60-80 pounds of stored honey to sustain bees through winter. Monitor food levels, and feed supplemental sugar syrup if needed before the weather turns cold. Hard candy boards can also provide emergency winter food.

Ensure the queen is actively laying eggs through fall to generate a healthy winter bee population. These heartier, longer-lived bees will maintain the colony into next spring. Watch for signs of a failing queen and replace if necessary heading into winter.

Treat hives for Varroa mites in late summer/early fall using options like formic acid, oxalic acid, or Apivar strips. Knock down mite levels to prevent them compromising bees' winter health. Screen bottom boards and drone brood trapping can also help control mites pre-winter.

Remove any empty supers from hives by early fall so bees consolidate into the bottom brood chamber, keeping it warmer. Ensure the hive has proper ventilation to prevent harmful moisture build-up over winter. Prop the cover up slightly, use a moisture board, or drill holes in the top.

Insulate hives to conserve bees' heat and energy stores. Wrap top and sides with tar paper, insulation boards, bales of straw, or other insulating materials suited to winter extremes in your area. Secure any wraps firmly.

Tilt hives forward slightly so any moisture drains out the entrance rather than pooling on the bottom board. Elevate hives on stands to improve winter air circulation and reduce ground moisture. Face entrances away from prevailing winds.

Secure entrance reducers in fall so mice and other pests can't access hives while allowing bees to ventilate. Monitor pollen patties and sugar syrup, removing any that could mold over winter. Install entrance guards or mouse screens to deter rodents.

In severely cold climates, some beekeepers move hives into unheated structures like barns or sheds. This adds a layer of protection from wind, ice, and dramatic temperature swings. Make sure to provide sufficient ventilation.

Check on hives periodically through winter. Observe entrance activity on warm days and see if ice needs removing. Refresh emergency food supplies if needed, taking care not to chill the cluster inside. Insulation wraps may need fortifying after strong winds or storms.

When spring's warm days return, carefully observe activity levels in hives that overwintered. Remove insulation slowly as temperatures rise to avoid shocking bees with sudden fluctuations. Feed bees thin sugar syrup to replenish food stores and stimulate brood production as the colony rebounds.

In summary, the key steps to winter prep are:

- Confirm adequate honey reserves 60-80 lbs
- Ensure a healthy queen and winter bee population
- Treat for mites and reduce infestations
- Consolidate down to lower boxes, removing empty supers
- Provide ventilation while sealing entrance gaps
- Insulate hive tops and sides appropriately
- Tilt hives forward for drainage
- Add entrance reducers and guards against pests
- Monitor food and activity throughout winter
- Remove insulation gradually as spring returns

Taking proper seasonal care prepares your hive for the demands of winter. Your dedication will be rewarded with healthy, vigorously renewed bee colonies ready for the opportunities of spring.

Roberta Bird

CHAPTER 5

THE LIFE CYCLE OF BEES

The Role of the Queen Bee

The queen bee is the very heart of a honey bee colony. There can only be one queen per hive. She alone performs the essential function of laying fertilized eggs to propagate the colony. The queen's health and prolificacy directly impact the productivity and survival of the entire colony. Understanding the multifaceted role of the queen provides critical insight for beekeepers.

On a biological level, the queen differs in several key ways from her sterile female worker sisters. Her abdomen is elongated to accommodate a fully developed reproductive system. She has an enlarged thorax to support her heavier body weight. The queen's stinger contains fewer barbs, allowing her to sting repeatedly without injury. She emits distinct pheromones that regulate social behaviors and colony cohesion. Physiologically and morphologically specialized for reproduction, the queen exists to lay eggs.

Queens develop from genetically identical female larvae that are fed a special diet of royal jelly. This triggers the full development of reproductive organs that remain stunted in worker larvae. Just before emergence, queen cells are constructed vertically from surrounding comb so she can execute her nuptial flight. Once mated, the queen will never leave the hive again except with a prime swarm.

Mating occurs during nuptial flights early in the queen's life. She will take multiple orientation flights, then mate in mid-air with 10-20 drones from other colonies. The semen collected during these flights is stored in her spermatheca organ to fertilize eggs for life. An unfertilized queen cannot successfully reign.

Once mated, the queen's primary role is efficiently laying fertilized eggs into wax cells. She will lay up to 1500 eggs per day at a rate of 1-2 eggs per minute! Fertilized eggs hatch into females—either queens or workers depending on diet. Unfertilized eggs become male drone bees. The queen also releases queen mandibular pheromone, which suppresses ovarian development in workers and identifies the queen's presence.

The queen will lay in a consistent pattern, starting from the center of the frame and spiraling outward. Dense, compact brood patterns reveal a healthy, vigorous queen. Spotty patterns signal potential issues with her performance. Queens typically continue laying for 1-3 years before their productivity declines.

When queen fertility falters, workers will respond by constructing emergency queen cells to replace her. The colony may also begin laying drone brood in worker cells, which can signal queen failure. Poor egg-laying patterns, a depleted queen pheromone, injury or disease all compromise her functionality. Identifying when the queen is failing allows beekeepers to requeen promptly before the colony is negatively impacted.

While the queen lays the eggs, workers tend to all aspects of brood rearing. Young workers feed thousands of hungry larvae. They maintain the proper hive temperature for brood development. Older workers cap cells when pupation begins. Some workers even remove sick or infested larvae to ensure healthy brood. This shows the interdependence between queen and workers for reproductive success.

Yet workers do sometimes establish queen cells to replace even healthy queens. This reproductive competition leads to swarming. When overcrowding occurs, the old queen leaves with roughly half the workers to establish a new nest site. The most mature queen cell then hatches in the original hive. The colony reproduces rather than collapses from congestion. But swarming leads to reduced honey production, so beekeepers try to prevent it through strategic splits.

Another key relationship exists between the queen and drones. On her mating flights, the queen will only mate with drones from distant colonies. This promotes genetic diversity in the hive. Yet drones do not contribute to colony functioning after mating. In fall when resources decline, workers evict drones from the hive to conserve food.

The queen also interacts with her sister queens in intriguing ways. When two queens emerge in a hive simultaneously, they will duel to the death until only one remains. Yet when queens meet as strangers, they are often surprisingly tolerant. Beekeepers utilize this trait when combining hives or introducing purchased queens. Still, rival queens sometimes kill one another, so queens are best kept separated.

Through her complex relationships with workers, drones, and sister queens, the queen bee orchestrates colony reproduction and productivity. Her presence supplies the necessary pheromones for social cohesion. Her egg laying propagates the hive's population. And her mating flights bring crucial genetic diversity. Despite workers performing the labor, the queen truly powers the colony as the central mother figure.

In summary, the queen forms the cornerstone of colony function and welfare. Her reproductive capacity directly enables the hive to thrive. Understanding the queen's biology and her dynamic interactions within the colony provides beekeepers with crucial insights. Learning to identify queen issues early allows appropriate intervention to maintain a healthy queen. Supporting the queen ultimately supports the colony as a whole. The bees work hard to promote and protect their queen, for they all rely on her continued success.

The Role of Worker Bees

Worker bees perform the vast majority of tasks essential to colony functioning. As female bees, they carry out every job in the hive except mating and laying eggs. A worker bee progresses through different roles as she ages, mastering the skills needed in each stage of her approximately 6 week life. Coordinating the collective work of thousands of workers enables a colony to grow, produce honey stores, and care for its members. Understanding the progression and responsibilities of worker bees provides insight into the social order of the hive.

Worker bees begin life as an egg. Once hatched, young workers spend their first few days as house bees cleaning brood cells in preparation for new eggs. After cell cleaning, workers act as nurse bees tending to larvae and the queen. Nurse bees feed thousands of hungry larvae each day, secreting nutritious jelly from glands in their heads. Meticulous care and feeding enables larvae to fully develop. Nurse bees also closely attend to the queen, grooming her and feeding her royal jelly to stimulate egg laying. Their diligent nurturing duties allow rapid colony expansion.

Middle-aged workers transition from caring for the youngest to feeding older members. As hive bees, they provide food and water to larvae getting ready to pupate and emerging adult bees. Hive bees process the nectar foragers collect into cured honey for colony consumption or surplus storage. They convert pollen into bee bread to feed the brood and adults. Through meticulous food storage, preparation, and distribution, hive bees provision the entire colony.

Guarding the hive entrance is another duty of middle-aged workers. Guards use their acute sense of smell to identify robbers from other colonies. They respond fearlessly in defense of their home, stinging threats unhesitatingly. Guards also regulate hive ventilation and temperature by fanning the entrance and controlling traffic flow. Their protective role keeps the colony secure.

In a worker bee's final weeks of life, she progresses to foraging outside the hive. Foragers collect nectar, pollen, propolis and water to supply the colony's needs. Intensive foragingstrain wears down the wings and body. Yet each load of provisions sustains the hive. Scout bees also search out new resource locations and communicate findings to other foragers. The efforts of this workforce gather the materials needed for nourishment, growth and defense.

Coordinating the concurrent activities of thousands of workers in various developmental stages enables a colony to thrive. Precise signals and cues compel workers to perform required tasks without active management. The queen's pheromones telegraph colony needs. For example, a decline in her "footprint" pheromones informs workers to switch from foraging to brood rearing. Food sharing by mouth communicates type and location of resources. The transfer of pollen from older to younger bees compels them to start expressing necessary glandular secretions for their upcoming roles. Stimuli from the state of the hive impels workers into action.

However, worker behavior also displays complex flexibility beyond reflexive responses. Workers collectively assess hive conditions and needs to allocate labor accordingly. When the queen is absent or failing, workers rear emergency queen cells to replace her. When food stores run low, more bees activate as foragers. Cooler temperatures trigger tighter clustering. This cognitive awareness of circumstances allows dynamic work allocation. Yet intrinsic preferences still drive role inclinations - young bees naturally favor nursing while older bees gravitate toward foraging. The interplay between worker bee instincts, age-related tendencies, and colony requirements underpins the elaborate division of labor.

While each worker performs specific tasks, the collective work output enables colony-level functioning. A solitary worker bee has a lifespan of just weeks. Yet the brood they nurture lives on, including new generations of workers. The honey they store can sustain the colony indefinitely. The comb they build outlasts them as a structural foundation. No single bee completes these larger goals alone. Lifetime service from waves of short-lived workers achieves the lasting productivity of the superorganism. Their unified purpose creates collective outcomes greater than the sum of individual lifetime contributions.

Understanding the nature and progression of worker tasks provides deeper insight into the coordinated workings of a honey bee colony. Knowing normal worker behaviors allows beekeepers to spot problems when activity seems abnormal. Providing the conditions that enable workers to perform their natural functions optimally - proper space, nutrition, population balance - allows the hive to thrive. Appreciating the essential, interconnected work performed by each generation of workers fosters respect and care for these industrious insects we rely upon.

The Role of Drones

Drone bees play a critical reproductive role in the colony. As male honey bees, drones have some key biological and behavioral differences from the females. Understanding the purpose and life cycle of drones provides insight into honey bee colony dynamics and health.

Physically, drones are stouter with broader abdomens compared to the tapered shape of worker bees. Their eyes are extra large, covering most of the head, to better spot and pursue queen bees during mating flights. Drones also have no pollen baskets on their hind legs or stingers for defense. Their sole purpose is reproductive.

Drones develop from unfertilized eggs laid by the queen. They hatch after 24 days, a full week longer than worker bees, since they develop more slowly. Drones weigh about twice as much as workers upon emerging as adults. Unlike female bees, drones do not possess the anatomical structures to collect nectar or pollen. They cannot participate in cooperative hive tasks.

Because they cannot directly contribute to the colony, drones require significant feeding by worker bees to survive. Workers regurgitate food to sustain them. A drone's diet consists of honey, pollen and royal jelly. This substantial nourishment cost means colonies typically limit drone production unless food sources are abundant.

Despite requiring such intensive feeding, drones are vital to the colony's reproduction. When a virgin queen emerges, she will embark on mating flights with drones. These take place about 5-10 days into her adult life. She mates mid-flight with multiple drones, who die shortly after mating.

The queen stores the male drones' genetic material inside her body. It is gradually released to fertilize eggs over the next few years of her life. The diversity of drone fathers helps maintain the colony's genetic health.

When resources within the hive become scarce, the colony reduces its drone population to conserve resources. Workers evict drones from the hive en masse or simply stop feeding them. The drones quickly die off during this process. The worker bees are essentially deciding to privilege the colony's survival over its reproduction until conditions improve.

The presence and quantity of drones offer key insights for beekeepers:

- Drones indicate the queen has been successfully mating.
- Abundant drones show plentiful food stores in the colony.
- Minimal drones suggest the queen may be compromised or infertile.
- Dead drones may indicate insufficient food resources.
- Seeing egg-laying by workers signals a failing or absent queen.

Monitoring drones throughout the active season provides clues about the queen's health and the hive's resource levels. It helps beekeepers ensure issues get addressed promptly.

The ongoing dance between reproduction and productivity plays out through the drones' treatment by the colony. Their existence is a delicate balance of resource drain and genetic contribution. While seemingly expendable as individuals, collectively drones are essential for sustaining the hive population.

By understanding the purpose and seasonal population dynamics of drones, beekeepers gain valuable perspective into events within the colony. Providing adequate food resources allows colonies to benefit from the genetic diversity drones facilitate. Supporting the reproductive role of drones helps promote ongoing hive health and renewal.

In summary, key points about drones include:

- Drones hatch from unfertilized queen eggs, requiring 24 days.
- They are physically distinct from female bees with larger eyes and size.
- Drones do not collect pollen or nectar and rely on worker feeding.
- They mate with the queen mid-flight, dying shortly after.
- Drones pass diverse genetics to the queen for egg fertilization.
- Colonies reduce drones when resources are scarce.
- Drone population indicates queen status and food reserves.
- Beekeepers monitor drones to gauge colony health.

By appreciating the reproductive contributions of drone bees, keepers can better interpret observations and support strong, productive hives.

Understanding Swarming

Swarming is a natural process of propagation and colony division in honey bee hives. When conditions are optimal, the hive will begin creating new queens and ultimately divide the colony in two. About half the workers leave with the old queen to establish a new nest site elsewhere. While swarming allows the colony to reproduce, it can also lead to a substantial loss of resources and bees for the beekeeper. Understanding what triggers swarm preparations, detecting signs early, and employing preventative tactics helps beekeepers minimize swarming events.

Swarming occurs as a response to prime colony conditions. When the hive is very strong in population, brood production, and food stores, the queen's pheromone becomes diluted. This triggers worker bees to start constructing several peanut-like queen cells, often on the bottom edges of frames. A virgin queen will develop in each cell as rivals.

Once the first of these queen cells is capped, preparations for swarm departure begin. Scouting bees search for suitable nesting cavity options outside the hive. The old queen diets down to shrink her abdomen in order to fly. A sub-group of workers also fills up on honey in preparation to leave. Within two weeks typically, the old queen exits with over half the worker population. This prime swarm relocates to the scouted nest site.

Several swarm stages follow in quick succession. First secondary swarms may leave with one or more newly emerged virgin queens. Later, one newly mated queen returns to the original hive and eliminates her unemerged sister queens by stinging their cells. A stable new laying queen then carries on in the primary location with the remaining bees.

For beekeepers, swarming leads to reduced honey production, loss of hive resources, and reproductive colonies to manage. Preventing swarming requires close vigilance and timely manipulations during spring and early summer when colonies are expanding rapidly. Regular inspections help catch queen cells early before swarms depart.

The key triggers that initiate swarming are congestion and a declining queen pheromone. Eliminating these factors allows halting the swarm impulse. Providing adequate living space stays ahead of expansion and avoids overcrowding. The brood nest should never fill more than eight frames; once the hive's population exceeds the cavity space, swarm instincts activate. Adding supers of empty drawn comb above a queen excluder as the hive grows satisfies the need for room.

Requeening with a fresh, young queen boosts the queen pheromone that suppresses swarm urges. Old queens nearing 2-3 years of age are more likely to be replaced. Requeening annually with a mated queen from a reputable breeder realigns the pheromone balance. Introduce the replacement queen using a queen cage to ensure safe, gradual acceptance.

Splits or divides are another method to prevent congestion and break the swarm impulse. The beekeeper divides one hive into two, providing a new queen for half the colony. This gives both halves ample room to thrive. Splits should be done during early signs of swarm preparation but before queen cells are capped. The hive can be split back together once expanded.

Destroying queen cells manually as soon as they appear also helps halt the sequence towards swarm departure. Check inside and underneath frames thoroughly for peanut-shaped cells, destroying any found by scooping them out. Leave only one cell intact as insurance if the queen then fails. Repeated cell destruction during spring disrupts the swarm mindset.

Providing adequate ventilation helps young queens better broadcast their scent through the hive, reducing the risk that workers will supersede her due to a weak pheromone. Reversing brood chambers can also concentrate the queen's output in a smaller area. Avoiding frequent disruptive inspections limits stress on the queen which could spur supersedure.

While swarms can be collected and hived, prevention is more productive for the beekeeper. Staying alert for early signs of congestion and queen cell construction allows prompt action. Maintaining living space, requeening, splitting, and culling cells redirects the colony's focus back to efficient brood rearing and honey production. With close monitoring and early mitigation tactics, most swarms can be avoided.

Of course, not all swarms can be fully prevented. Unexpected events like sudden population booms or queen events may still trigger swarm departures. Secondary afterswarms with virgin queens are especially prone to escape. Marking the queen makes her loss more obvious. Having spare equipment ready allows catching and hiving swarms for increase rather than loss.

In summary, swarming is a complex reproductive process initiated when prime colony conditions cause congestion and declining queen pheromone. While the colony is responding naturally, swarming does reduce productivity. Beekeepers must remain vigilant for early signs like queen cells. Relieving congestion, requeening, splitting, and destroying cells can redirect the hive's focus. With attentive hive management and swift responses, most swarms can be averted. Though challenging, staying a step ahead of swarm preparation is key to maintaining strong and stable honey production colonies.

The Importance of Pollination

Pollination is a vital ecological process whereby pollen is transferred between flowering plants to enable fertilization and reproduction. Bees play an essential role as pollinators, carrying pollen from bloom to bloom as they collect nectar and pollen for food. Understanding the mechanics and importance of pollination provides critical insight into the indispensable contributions honey bees make to natural ecosystems and agriculture.

Pollination occurs when pollen grains move between flowers of the same species. Some plant species self-pollinate, where pollen transfers from male anthers to female stigmas within a single flower or between flowers on one plant. But the majority of flowering plants depend on cross-pollination between separate individuals to form seeds and fruit. Pollen must be delivered from an anther on one plant to a stigma on a genetically distinct individual of the same species for successful cross-fertilization.

Bees efficiently facilitate this cross-pollination as they visit multiple flowers gathering nectar and pollen. Their hairy bodies easily pick up dry pollen grains. As they crawl into each blossom, some pollen brushes off onto the sticky stigmas while new pollen adheres. Foraging from plant to plant enables this vital pollen transfer between compatible mates. Research shows bees can distribute viable pollen several miles from its source. This biodiverse pollen sharing strengthens the gene pool.

Pollination is essential for flowering plant reproduction and genetic diversity. Pollen deposited on stigmas travels down style tubes to fertilize ovules, forming seeds that carry the next generation. Cross-pollination increases genetic variation, improving the species' resilience and adaptability. Resulting seed and fruit production provides food for myriad animals up the food chain. Pollination underpins the continuity of plant populations in ecosystems.

In agricultural settings, bee pollination dramatically boosts yields and quality of many crops. Squash, apples, cherries, almonds and other plants require pollen transfer to bear marketable fruit. Insufficient pollination causes misshapen or stunted produce. Environmentally controlled greenhouse production often necessitates manually pollinating by hand. But open field crops rely fully on insect pollinators for the quantity and quality needed for profitable harvests. Managed honey bees play a major role fertilizing these crops.

The mechanics of honey bee pollination reveal their outstanding efficacy. As bees suck nectar from blossoms, dehiscing anthers deposit pollen grains onto their bodies. Backward-facing hairs enable excellent pollen collection. Foraging from plant to plant results in pollen depositing on the next flower's stigma as the bee penetrates deeply seeking nectar. Bees preferentially visit flowers of the same species during each foraging trip, enabling productive cross-pollination. Flower shape and chemistry guide bees to enter blossoms in ways that maximize pollen transfer. This pollination symbiosis between plants and bees coevolved over millions of years.

Understanding the pollination needs of specific crops improves orchard and field layouts. Different crops have varying pollination requirements and bloom periods. Some fruit trees are self-fruitful while others require cross-pollinator trees interspersed between rows. Planting alternate rows of different varieties promotes good pollen exchange. Crops like squash needing heavy bee visitation should be clustered near hives. Sequentially blooming orchard underplantings or cover crops extend the duration of pollinator sustaining forage. Though bees move pollen miles, purposeful farm planning utilizes their services most effectively.

In both natural and agricultural settings, healthy bee populations are essential for sufficient pollination. Habitat loss, pesticides, parasites, disease and climate change overstress both managed and native pollinators. Supporting sustainable beekeeping, conserving wild habitat, banning neonicotinoids, and creating pollinator-friendly forage on private and public lands protects essential pollinators. Lack of bees would mean lack of fruits, nuts, seeds, and diversity in nature. The ecosystem services pollinators provide have immeasurable importance.

In summary, ongoing pollination by bees sustains plants that nourish wildlife, stabilize landscapes, and feed humans. The productivity of farms and gene flow in natural areas depend on bees transferring pollen from flower to flower. Attentive apiary management, conservation initiatives, and pollinator-focused agriculture policies are needed to ensure adequate bee populations. The joys of beekeeping go hand-in-hand with doing our part to support these creatures so vital to ecological and food production.

Roberta Bird

CHAPTER 6

THE ART OF BEEKEEPING

Beekeeping Seasons

Beekeeping tasks and hive priorities change with the seasons. Understanding the annual cycle of activity, growth, and decline allows you to align management practices accordingly. Tailoring your efforts by season both protects colonies in stressful times and takes advantage of productive periods.

Spring

The arrival of spring's warm weather, blossoms, and lengthening days reawakens the hive. The queen resumes laying eggs to rapidly expand the worker population. Feed bees thin sugar syrup or pollen patties to fuel growth. Add supers and hive bodies to accommodate the influx of nectar and bees. Monitor for swarm preparations and divide colonies if needed. Perform pest management and medication before populations peak. Install queen excluders for honey harvesting later in the season.

Summer

Colonies reach peak productivity in summer. Multiple hive bodies and supers accommodate the hive's expansion. Monitor honey storage levels and extract any excess. Manage swarming inclinations by providing ample space, dividing crowded hives, or replacing old queens. Continue mite treatments and pest control measures. Ensure adequate ventilation to prevent overheating. Add separate honey supers for extracting uncontaminated honey. Water sources help bees cool the hive.

Fall

As winter nears, hive priorities shift to rearing winter bees and storing food. Remove unneeded hive bodies to condense colonies but maintain adequate honey storage. Treat for mites and reduce populations. Feed 2:1 sugar syrup to boost winter food reserves if needed. Stop any queen rearing or swarm control. Remove honey supers once extracting is finished; the hive should retain their own food. Reduce hive entrances to keep out pests. Prep for winter by weatherizing hive components.

Winter

Overwintering bees rely on stored honey and pollen to survive until spring, clustering tightly to retain heat. Wind blocks, insulation, and tilted hives will protect them from the elements. Moisture control is important to avoid mold and chill. Entrance reducers keep the interior stable but ventilated. Avoid opening hives in extremely cold conditions. Quickly replace any emergency food depleted by the cluster. Monitor food levels on warm winter days when bees can exit to cleanse.

In warmer climates, bee populations may continue rearing brood at a reduced rate over winter. Provide supplementary protein and watch for new queen cells. Reduce and consolidate down to smaller hives to help retain heat if needed.

Tailoring your plans by season allows you to work in harmony with the hive's natural rhythms. Supporting their changing needs through the annual cycle will translate into healthy bees and bountiful honey harvests.

In summary, key seasonal focus areas are:

- Spring - population growth, swarm prevention, adding space
- Summer - maximizing production, extracting honey
- Fall - winter prep, mite management, condensing hive
- Winter - insulation, ventilation, emergency food provision

While each season brings distinct challenges and opportunities, diligent beekeepers can maintain thriving colonies year-round through conscientious seasonal management tailored to their climate and locale.

Managing Multiple Hives

Many beekeepers choose to start small with just a few hives as they learn. But often interest grows to manage a larger apiary of 10 or more colonies. Running multiple hives provides benefits but also requires additional tools, techniques, and time commitment. Key elements of successfully scaling up include strategic apiary layout, recordkeeping, routine inspection schedules, equalizing hives, and integrating new colonies. Thoughtful multi-hive management enables greater honey yields, easier wintering, and a fulfilling beekeeping experience.

Site layout is a top consideration when expanding beyond just a few hives. Hives should be positioned in rows facing the same direction with entrances clear of obstacles. Maintaining a consistent orientation prevents drifting where bees return to the wrong colony. Spacing hives farther apart in hot climates prevents crowding. Arrange the apiary so hives can be worked with minimum disruptive crossing in front.

Group weaker splits or nucleus colonies centrally within the apiary. Stronger, more populous hives should flank the outside as a defensive barrier. Rotate hive positions systematically each season to equalize effects of any location differences. Mark each hive with a unique name or number for quick identification. Paint color codes can also distinguish groups like production hives versus breeders.

Detailed recordkeeping becomes more essential with multiple hives. Logbooks track lineage, requeening dates, honey yields, pest and disease issues, temperament, wintering success and more. Date and label frames during inspections. Notequeen status, brood pattern, food stores, population size and health observations for each hive. Records enable selective breeding, troubleshooting, and comparing productivity between different lines.

Routine inspection schedules help ensure all colonies get timely monitoring. Aim for 7-10 day intervals during peak season, longer in winter. Quickly scan for eggs, larvae and food stores before detailed review. Systematically move frame-by-frame to find the queen. Compare colonies side-by-side for any lags. Catch issues early before they escalate. Rotate which hives get inspected first to mix up timing.

As hives expand at different rates, periodic equalizing prevents overly strong or weak colonies. Swap out frames of eggs, brood and food from robust hives to even out populousness. Combine weak hives using newspaper combines. Promote good traffic flow, ventilation and defensive positioning in all hives. Equalization reduces swarming and robbing issues.

Integrating new colonies requires care to prevent rejection. Proper introduction, ample food reserves and minimal early disruption help new hives settle in. Place nucs centrally within the apiary for protection. Monitor queens closely for acceptance. Feed all colonies when adding or replacing queens to prevent robbing. Rotate drawn comb from strong hives into establishing colonies. Handle all bees gently to avoid provoking defensiveness.

Certain procedures require assistance with multiple hives. Enlist a helper for heavy lifting tasks like honey supers. An extra pair of hands also speeds requeening, splitting, or moving hives. Experienced mentors can provide guidance inspecting and assessing larger apiaries. Joining a local bee club fosters relationships for mutual aid.

Scaling beyond just a couple hives brings rewarding benefits but also real time commitments. Periodic hive inspections, recordkeeping, feeding, monitoring for swarm cells, winter prep and other management tasks take more time with increased numbers of colonies. Larger honey harvests require more equipment for extraction and bottling. Consider realistic workload abilities in determining optimal apiary size.

Advantages of operating multiple hives include:

- Increased honey production with more bees gathering nectar
- Genetic diversity and ability to select prime breeders
- Backup colonies in case some fail
- Splitting resources like equipment and bees between hives
- Improved winter survival rates through shared warmth

But beware disadvantages like:

- Exponential increase in inspection/management time
- Higher costs for woodenware, medication, feed, etc.
- Storage space needed for excess honey supers
- Increased burden treating diseases or hive beetles
- More difficult transporting hives for pollination

Finding the ideal apiary size requires honesty about your time constraints, management preference, and ultimate beekeeping goals. Get support where needed, monitor diligently, and enjoy the rewards of more bountiful bees.

Splitting and Transferring Hives

Expanding your apiary often involves splitting robust colonies to form new hives or transferring bees between existing hives. Both techniques allow beekeepers to increase total colony numbers, prevent swarming, and bolster weak hives. With proper execution, splitting and transferring are useful management practices.

Splitting divides one hive into two or more separate colonies. It requires a large, healthy parent hive with adequate worker bees, brood, and resources to share. Avoid splitting weak or small hives. Time splits for early spring when the population is rapidly expanding but before swarm preparations escalate.

Start by identifying the original queen and isolating her temporarily in a nuc box or split chamber. Let the parent hive realize she is absent for 1-2 days so they start emergency queen cell production. Destroy any existing swarm cells they make in this time.

Once they have started new round queen cells, divide the parent hive's frames between the split and the original nest. Aim to allocate approximately half the bees, brood, and food evenly. Gently brush extra bees off crowded frames. Install new empty frames in any vacant space and close up both hives.

Return the original laying queen to parent hive box. One of the new queen cells in the split will emerge and mate, giving them a new local mated queen. Providing ample nurse bees in both halves will allow continuous brood rearing as the new queens establish.

Feed both portions and monitor food reserves, brood progress, and queen acceptance. Uniting or recombining is an option if the split fails. Once both hives are stable, the new addition will boost your apiary's productivity.

Transferring bees involves shifting frames from robust hives into weaker colonies. It helps equalize hive strength, especially in spring. Assess frames in strong hives for unused space, condensed brood patterns or backfilling with honey. This indicates they can spare resources.

Select a weaker hive to receive transferred frames. Move frames shake off some adhering bees. Avoid moving the queen. Insert these transferred frames in the center of the recipient hive's box, sandwiching them between existing combs.

If you move brood, the recipient colony will raise the young already present. Sharing food stores helps nourish smaller colonies. Adding bees bolsters the population to better regulate temperature and defend the hive.

Providing resources from robust hives supports growth of weaker ones. But only transfer surplus resources to avoid harming the donor hive. Balance strengthening and sustaining colonies across your apiary.

When executing transfers:

- Pick frames loaded with bees, brood, honey and pollen to move.
- Brush adhering bees back into the donor hive.
- Insert frames carefully into the center of the receiving hive.
- Avoid chilling brood while transferring.
- Equalize hives gradually over multiple sessions if needed.

With diligent monitoring, splitting and transferring allows you to expand your apiary, prevent swarming inclinations, and bolster struggling hives by redistributing resources where needed. Just take care to avoid spreading diseases between colonies in the process.

In summary, key points include:

- Split robust hives in early spring before swarming starts.
- Isolate the queen temporarily so they start queen cells.
- Divide bees, brood, and food resources evenly into two boxes.
- Transfer frames from strong hives to boost weaker colonies.
- Target frames with bees, brood, honey and pollen for moving.
- Insert transferred frames into the center of recipient hives.

- Balance strengthening small hives with sustaining large donors.

Attracting Bees to Your Garden

Inviting more pollinators like bees into your garden enhances productivity and biodiversity. Through thoughtful plant choices and habitat provisions, you can create an oasis of nourishment and shelter for bees. This mutually benefits your garden's health while also supporting local bee populations.

When designing bee-friendly gardens, strive for continuous bloom throughout the seasons. Include a diverse mix of annuals, perennials, trees, and shrubs that provide successive waves of blossoms from spring through fall. Native plants suited to your region tend to be richest in pollen and nectar. Herbs, vegetables, and fruit trees will also reward visiting bees.

Bees are drawn to flowers in shades of purple, blue, yellow, and white. Double-petaled varieties should be avoided, as bees cannot access their pollen and nectar. Plant shape also matters, with tubular and dish-shaped blossoms making it easiest for bees to feed. Target plants with open, loose petal formations.

Incorporate variety in height, growth habit, and bloom time to support different bee species. Mass groupings of the same flowers make efficient feeding stops. Allow foliage around plants to grow naturally as nesting spots. Limit pesticide use to prevent poisoning pollinators and contaminating their food source.

Beyond plants, providing clean water appeals to all bees. Shallow birdbaths, fountains, or ponds give bees access without risk of drowning. Mix in small stones for perches. Site water sources in sunny areas protected from wind. Keep water freshened routinely.

Supplement floral resources by cultivating adjoining areas of nesting habitat. Leave bare earth patches for ground-nesting bees. Build simple bee "hotels" by drilling various sized holes in wood blocks for cavity-nesters. position these in warm areas facing sunrise. Bundle dried stems or blocks with holes for leafcutter bees.

When establishing new plants, choose small starts instead of mature specimens. Young plants invest more energy into robust root systems, becoming more resilient. Plus, small starts are cheaper! Focus on native perennial plants suited to your climate. Select a variety of plants with different bloom seasons, heights, and forms.

Group new plants based on irrigation needs. Zone areas for high, moderate or low water together. Use drip irrigation where possible to minimize evaporation. Add 2-4 inches of organic mulch around plants to retain moisture and suppress weeds. Provide temporary shade for the first few weeks until they establish.

In the first year, remove any flowers to redirect energy to root and vegetative growth. Larger blossoms can stress small plants. Remove dead or diseased growth promptly. Weed regularly to reduce competition for young plants. Avoid fertilizing at planting time but provide a thin layer of compost or slow-release organic fertilizer around plants.

Most plants take 1-3 years to reach maturity and display their full form. Peruse nurseries for inspiration but evaluate mature sizes before buying. Give plants ample room to grow into their natural shape and spread. Follow spacing guidelines on plant tags.

Group plants thoughtfully by light and water needs. Place taller, spreading varieties towards the back or center. Leave ample walking paths between beds. Cluster pots or shorter plants towards the front for visibility and access.

To create a thriving, self-sustaining habitat, mimic nature by layering plants. Combine tall trees, medium shrubs, trailing vines, herbaceous perennials, annuals, grasses, and groundcovers. This diversity provides visual interest along with ecological benefits.

Bee-Friendly Plants

Providing an abundance of nutritious forage plants greatly benefits honey bee colonies. Certain flowering species provide the nectar and pollen bees rely on to produce honey and feed their brood. Landscaping with bee-friendly plants around hives and in the broader landscape allows bees to access diverse, ample nutrition.

When selecting bee plants, flowering perennials are ideal. Unlike annuals that bloom briefly, robust perennials offer recurring nourishment year after year. Native wildflower perennials suited to your bioregion tend to be most beneficial. Native plants that formed co-evolutionary relationships with local pollinators offer bees specialized adaptations in their flowers. Prioritize native species over exotic ornamentals for optimal forage value.

Target plants that bloom at different times to supply food continuity through spring, summer and fall. For example, early bloomers like willows provide an abundant pollen source when colonies are expanding in spring. Summer stalwarts like purple coneflowers and black-eyed Susans extend peak foraging through mid-season. Asters, goldenrods and other fall flowers supply nutrients before winter dormancy. Staggered bloom periods prevent seasonal forage gaps.

Based on your climate, aim for diversity in flower colors, shapes and species. Generalist bees visit a wide spectrum of plant families versus specialized relationships. Massing multiple plants of a given species makes their floral rewards more apparent. But planting many species compensates for variations in individual plants' productivity year-to-year. A diverse floral buffet supports balanced bee nutrition and general colony health.

Here are some top perennial plant picks for small-scale gardens up to acres:

- Wildflowers: asters, coneflowers, sunflowers, milkweed, ironweed, joe pye weed, goldenrods, bergamot, penstemon, vervain, violets, asters, geraniums, phacelia

- Herbs and vegetables: lavender, thyme, rosemary, oregano, basil, dill, fennel, cilantro, parsley, cabbage, broccoli

- Shrubs and vines: blueberry, raspberry, serviceberry, sumac, willow, clematis, trumpet vine

- Trees: maple, willow, basswood, tuliptree, locust, redbud, apple, cherry, plum, citrus

When evaluating bee plants, pay attention to flower structure. Shallow, accessible flowers with landing platforms make nectar and pollen easy to reach. Tubular blooms tend to favor longer-tongued bees, though some bumblebees can "nectar rob" by chewing holes. Avoid doubled flowers, as extra petals block pollinator access. Single, open blooms are best.

Be mindful that some supposedly bee-friendly exotic plants can become overly aggressive or invasive. Always consult local native plant societies before introducing non-native species. Even some natives like milkweeds may require management to prevent excessive spread. Carefully balance biodiversity with responsible stewardship.

For planted rows or flower bed blocks, arrange plants closely in clumps rather than scattered. Dense masses of a given species help bees locate bountiful resources. However, avoid creating single-species monocultures devoid of bloom diversity. A mosaic of plant clusters provides bees the variety they need.

Supplementing flowers with nesting habitats also supports bees. Leave bare soil patches where ground-nesting native bees can burrow. Ensure gradual sunlight exposures without sudden high-heat windows. Avoid applying thick mulch that deters ground-nesting. Brush piles, fallen logs with tunnels, and bamboo stems create refuge for above-ground cavity nesters. Planting bee pastures through considered selection and arrangements allows everyone to thrive.

In summary, purposeful landscaping with bee-nourishing flowers makes a measurable impact on colony productivity. Seeking out native perennials, providing seasonal continuity, and emphasizing non-invasive varieties provides ecological integrity. Parkways, backyard gardens, urban planters, window boxes, farms, and meadows can all contribute sustenance at various scales. With conscientious plant choices and placements, we can lend bees a helping hand through thoughtful forage provisioning in any landscape.

BONUS 1

AUDIOBOOK

Scan the QR code and access the audiobook

Roberta Bird

BONUS 2

VIDEO

Scan the QR code

Roberta Bird

EXCLUSIVE BONUS

3 EBOOK

Scan the QR code or click the link and access the bonuses

http://subscribepage.io/jh0ljb

Roberta Bird

AUTHOR BIO
ROBERTA BIRD

R oberta Bird, a seasoned author whose life seamlessly blends the world of beekeeping with the practicalities of her work in a sports goods store. With over two decades invested in the art of beekeeping, Roberta's journey began as a laid-back hobby, eventually evolving into a genuine passion and profession.

By day, she's engaged in the sports retail industry, assisting customers and managing inventory. Yet, her afternoons transform into a buzzing hive of activity as she tends to beehives, keenly observing the intricate lives of her favorite insects.

Roberta's family plays a crucial role in her story, sharing the excitement of honey harvesting and the satisfaction of discovering thriving hives. As a devoted mother and partner, she creates memorable moments in the garden, surrounded by the diligent hum of her buzzing companions.

Roberta Bird

Printed in Great Britain
by Amazon